Luis Muñoz Marín

THE MAN WHO REMADE PUERTO RICO

by Peggy Mann

Coward, McCann & Geoghegan, Inc. New York

Photo credits

Dr. Antonio Colorado, 62 top, right

Commonwealth of Puerto Rico, jacket photo; 62 bottom, right and left

Ruth Gruber, 63 bottom, right and left

Puerto Rico Information Service, 4; 62 top, left

Jacket photo, courtesy of the
Commonwealth of Puerto Rico

 Published simultaneously in Canada by Longman Canada Limited, Toronto.

SBN: GB 698-30614-7

SBN: TR 698-20362-3

Library of Congress Cataloging in Publication Data

Mann, Peggy.

Muñoz Marín: the man who remade Puerto Rico.

Bibliography: p.

Includes index.

SUMMARY: A biography of the man responsbile for transforming Puerto Rico from an island of poverty, disease, and squalor into "the Showplace of the Caribbean."

1. Muñoz Marín, Luis, 1898- —Juvenile literature. 2. Puerto Rico—Politics and government—1952- —Juvenile literature. [1. Muñoz Marín, Luis, 1898- 2. Puerto Rico—Biography] I. Title.

F1976.M76M26 1976 972.95'05'0924 [B] [92] 76-6117

PRINTED IN THE UNITED STATES OF AMERICA

For

Dr. Antonio Colorado

CHAPTER 1

"Well," said the clerk in a fake-friendly voice, "I put you down as Joe Rivera, okay?"

"Why?" asked Luisito. "That's not my name."

The clerk held up the registration form which the boy had just filled out. "You expect me to write all this on all your records: Luis José Alberto Muñoz Marín?"

"For short, I'm Luis," the boy said. "Not Joe!"

"Look, son," the clerk said. "No need to get your dander up. I'm just trying to make things easier for you. You're entering here midterm—the only Puerto Rican boy in the class. Things'll be hard enough for you as it is. I know thirteen-year-old boys. And let me tell you, son, the motto is: Don't be different! Now, the first place to start is with your name. So—we'll put you down as *Louis* Rivera. All right?"

"My last name is Muñoz," Luisito said. "Not Rivera."

The clerk frowned. "Wasn't that your father who just left here?"

The boy nodded.

"He told me his name was Senior Moonose Rivera."

"MooNYOZ Rivera," said Luisito, "Not Moonose."

"Okay," said the clerk, "MooNYOZ Rivera. So if *his* name's Rivera, why isn't yours?"

"My last name is Muñoz," the boy said wearily. He had been through this many times in the last six months. "My *full* last name is Muñoz Marín. Marín is the maiden name of my mother. Rivera is the maiden name of my father's mother. *His* last name is Muñoz, too. Or Muñoz Rivera. But what his last name is *not* is Rivera. That's the way they make names in Spanish countries."

"Wait a minute, young fellow," the clerk said. "If someone asks you a simple question like 'What's your name?' and you start sounding off about the maiden name of your father's mother, they'll think you're a little—" He tapped his forehead significantly.

"Forget it!" Luisito said. "Call me what you want!"

He realized suddenly that this man probably felt sorry for him and was trying to be kind. And he was probably wondering what kind of father would bring his son in here to the Administration Office and then rush right out. Probably the clerk did not know that his father was the great Muñoz Rivera—Puerto Rico's resident commissioner to the Congress of the United States. The very busy resident commissioner, who had to hurry off to an important Congressional meeting and could not even stay to see his son's new room, his son's new world.

"Where'd you learn your English?" asked the clerk. "You have no accent at all."

"I grew up in New York City," Luis told him. "At least I was there from the time I was three until I was eight.

Then we went back home to Puerto Rico.'' It was a nice sentence to say: *Then we went back home*. Now there was no more "we." His parents were separated. And there was no more home. Not for him anyway. His home would be a room in a dorm in Georgetown Prep, in Washington, D.C.

"Well, young fellow," said the clerk, handing him a yellow card, "here's your room assignment."

"Thanks," Luisito said. On the card was the name of a dormitory: Healy Hall. There was a room number, and his name printed in ink: JOE RIVERA. He picked up his suitcase and went to the door.

"Good luck," the clerk said. He did not add: *You'll need it*. But the boy sensed that the words were there.

He went slowly down the steps of the Administration Building and walked across the red brick courtyard framed by fine old brick buildings. Boys hurried past him, talking and laughing. Everyone else seemed to know someone; everyone else belonged.

Perhaps he would have a roommate his age; a boy who would help him find his way into this new world.

But the room in Healy Hall which had been assigned to Joe Rivera was large enough to hold a cot, a chest of drawers, a desk, and a chair. And that was all.

He closed the door behind him and started to unpack. Amid a jumble of shirts, pajamas, and underwear he found the silver-framed portrait of his mother and put it on the bare bureau top. Looking at her picture, he suddenly knew—he had made a mistake. He should have stayed with his mother in New York City. So what if the public school on Seventy-second Street was not as fine as Georgetown Prep—at least PS 84 was free. And he wasn't the only Puerto Rican in the school. And they called him by his own name—Luis Muñoz Marín—not Joe Rivera! But the most important thing about the last six months had been his mother: the beautiful, brilliant, witty Doña Amalia. Now he could only see her on weekends, if at all.

Six months before, when Luis Muñoz Rivera, the newly elected resident commissioner, had left Puerto Rico to take his new job in Washington, D.C., it had been decided that thirteen-year-old Luisito should henceforth live in Manhattan with his mother.

Luisito adored his mother. And loved Manhattan. The memories he'd made there as a small boy were good ones. Sleigh riding in Central Park. Watching dinosaurlike cranes and steam shovels dig the huge subway cavern at Broadway and 103rd. Going with his papá to baseball games at the Polo Grounds, then sitting on the stoop steps describing the game, inning by inning, to his friend Dutchie. (Their special hero was the Giants' catcher, an American Indian, Chief Meyers.) And Coney Island—his favorite place: Luna Park, Dream Land, the Loop de Loop. Whenever his parents wanted his "full cooperation" that was the lure. ("Be good at the dentist's and we'll take you to Coney Island.")

It *had* been "we" then. They were a family. Even though they moved frequently, wherever they lived was home. Because they were together: Papá, Mamá, and Luisito.

When they first arrived in Manhattan they had taken a room at the Chelsea Hotel on Twenty-third Street—where the desk clerk gave three-year-old Luisito his first English lessons. Then they moved to a Spanish boardinghouse on Sixty-fourth Street, a run-down block between Amsterdam and Columbus avenues. As the *Puerto Rico Herald*—the newspaper founded by Muñoz Rivera—began to do better, the family moved again. And again. Always in Manhattan, always on the West Side, always together.

But it would not be that way anymore.

When he'd left to come to Georgetown Prep, Doña Amalia had made it quite clear that she would never set foot in Washington, D.C. If her son wanted to see her he must return to 64 West 110th Street. There he would always have a room waiting.

But despite his mother's pleas that he remain with her, Luisito had given in to the arguments of his papá. Which was why he now found himself all alone at Georgetown Prep. His father's suite at the Benedict Apartment Hotel was ten miles away. And there was no room in it for Luisito. When he stayed with Papá he would have to sleep on the couch.

Papá.

He should, by rights, have brought a picture of his father to put on the bureau next to that of his mother. After all, a picture of his papá hung in shops, restaurants, public buildings, and schools throughout all of Puerto Rico.

For as long as Luisito could remember, his father had been the most important man on the island. They called him El León, the Lion. Or "the George Washington of Puerto Rico." And six months previously, when he was elected resident commissioner, the island's only representative to the American Congress, Luis Muñoz Rivera had become more important than ever.

This, perhaps, was why Luisito had not brought a picture of Papá with him.

Even in the Manhattan public school he'd just come from, he had been known as the son of Luis Muñoz Rivera. But here, for the first time in his life, he would be just another student. Luis Muñoz. Or Joe Rivera. Here he would make it, or not. But whatever happened, it would have nothing to do with his father's name.

CHAPTER 2

As the months went by, Luisito began to realize that perhaps he had not made a mistake by coming to Georgetown.

It was not that he did very well in school. Most of the teachers were Jesuit priests, and he found these black-cassocked fathers rather forbidding. He was used to the easy informality of the private school he had gone to in Puerto Rico; students of all ages met in the same huge high-ceilinged room in Pedro Moczo's blue-painted house in old San Juan. It was said of Don Pedro: "He doesn't know grades; he just knows knowledge." And in that informal atmosphere Luisito learned so much that now in Georgetown Prep he had been put into classes with fourteen- and fifteen-year-old boys. This, of course, did not make it any easier for him to find friends at Georgetown, and he was lonely.

Nevertheless he was glad he had come to Georgetown—because of his papá. Muñoz Rivera was as busy as he had always been. Yet now, for the first time, he set aside special time to be with his son. Every Sunday they would eat in a restaurant and then return to the apartment, where the resident commissioner worked on papers and speeches and Luisito did his homework. And then—the part of the day the boy liked best and looked forward to all week—they gave each other lessons.

The assignments which Muñoz Rivera doled out to his son might be on any subject which struck his fancy at the moment. One Sunday it was "Look up the Punic Wars in the encyclopedia." The next Sunday: "Translate this article on Goya from French into Spanish." He was a good teacher. He'd had practice. His mother had died when he was twelve, and he had taken on the job of tutoring his nine younger brothers and sisters. Now, with one boy to teach instead of nine—and with a half century of learning and experience to impart—Luis Muñoz Rivera opened countless new worlds to his son and made them crackle with excitement.

But for Luisito the most exciting time of all came when he was the teacher and his father the student. The subject was English conversation. It was the one area in which the son knew far more than the father.

During the eight years Muñoz Rivera had lived in Manhattan as founder and editor of the *Puerto Rico Herald,* he had learned very little English. His paper was printed in Spanish and English. He wrote in Spanish and had his articles translated into English. He spoke Spanish at work and at home with Amalia and Luisito. There was no real need for him to be fluent in English.

Now, however, Muñoz Rivera faced quite a different situation. Although the resident commissioner was not permitted to vote in the U.S. Congress, he was permitted to speak. Indeed, he was expected to speak—he was the sole official voice of all the Puerto Ricans on the island:

one man to speak for a million people, the majority of whom were unemployed, illiterate, disease-ridden, and without hope.

However, in order to speak, to journalists, to Congressmen, and to President Wilson, Luis Muñoz Rivera needed to learn English—in a hurry. During the first six months in Washington he had bought himself a grade-school English grammar book and a set of "Easy English" records which he played on his Victrola. In a firm, ringing voice he announced to the walls: "We are having beautiful weather," or he asked with the proper interested expression: "What is the price of a dozen eggs?"

But these were not the phrases he would need when addressing Congressmen about the dire plight of the Puerto Rican people.

Therefore, Luisito was pressed into service as a professor of English conversation. And a strict teacher he was. He loved scolding his papá, putting him through his paces. And, finally, complimenting him. "That's very good, Papá. You sounded like an American—almost."

And Muñoz Rivera would laugh, delighted—with himself and with his son.

Like any good language teacher, Luisito selected subjects which were of keen interest to his pupil. And the subjects were of keen interest to the teacher as well—for Muñoz Rivera often figured as the chief character.

"Tell me, Papá," Professor Luisito would say, "about the time you tracked down Sagasta on the Spanish beach."

And, falteringly, in his best "Easy English," Muñoz

Rivera would launch into the tale which climaxed in his well-known title: "the George Washington of Puerto Rico."

Puerto Rico had belonged to Spain ever since Columbus first landed on the island in 1493. By the time Luis Muñoz Rivera became editor of his own newspaper, *La Democracia*, in 1890, the island was rumbling with rebellion. Only Cuba and Puerto Rico were left as remnants of Spain's once-mighty empire in the Western Hemisphere. And Puerto Rico wanted to rule itself.

"In 1895," Muñoz Rivera recounted slowly, "I have thirty-six years. I tell I am badly of health, so I must to cure me have an ocean trip—to Spain." He laughed loudly and winked at his son.

Luisito corrected his father's sentence and then asked, "Did Mamá go with you?"

"Of course!" Muñoz Rivera roared. "We have two year of married only. She is a very beauty. You think I leave her home?"

The editor and his "very-beauty" wife had spent a busy five months in Spain meeting politicians, looking for allies in the forthcoming fight for self-government in Puerto Rico (and attending a number of glamorous parties). He returned home knowing more about Spanish politics than anyone else on the island. And the following year he insisted that an official four-man commission be sent to Spain. It was, Muñoz Rivera reasoned, a good time to go, for Cuba was fighting a war against Spain. Perhaps the Spanish leaders would give Puerto Rico self-government, rather than fight two wars at the same time.

"But maybe was *not* so good time to go to Madrid!"

Muñoz Rivera remembered with another laugh. "Was summertime. Very, very hot in Madrid. All the Spanish leaders—zum—they left the city. So—zum—I left the city too. I take a train to the beaches. I look for them."

On a beach in Andalusia he had found Práxedes Sagasta in his bathing suit. Sagasta was the leader of the Spanish Liberal Party.

"That party," said Muñoz Rivera, "was out. But I win from Sagasta the promise that if he get again in, he give self-rule to Puerto Rico. Fine. Good, I think. But when I come home, people laugh at me. Why, they say, not I win agreement from the leader who is in? But," and a smile spread across his face, "one year later, what is happen?"

"The man who was *in*," Luisito shouted, "was shot dead. So he was out. And Sagasta was in. And *you* were in, Papá!" He knew the story well, of course. It was written in detail in all Puerto Rican history books. But reading it there was not quite the same as hearing the tale told—in English—by its hero.

Sagasta, the new Spanish premier, true to his promise to Muñoz Rivera, had given Puerto Rico self-rule, with its own elected parliament which would make all laws for the island. Spain would have a say only in matters of foreign affairs. The island's first free election was held. And Luis Muñoz Rivera—the man who had won Puerto Rico's freedom, with words not war—became the island's first premier. He took office on February 8, 1898.

"And ten days later," said Muñoz Rivera, pointing a finger at his son, "you is born. And five month later—

zum—I am no more premier. And Puerto Rico is again a colony. This time a colony of the USA!"

It had happened so fast that no one quite knew what had happened. Or why.

In 1895 Spain had sent troops to put down the Cuban rebellion, and did so by imprisoning hundreds of thousands of Cubans behind barbed wire fences, where they died of disease and starvation. New York newspapers increased circulation by printing pictures and gory details about the suffering Cubans. And they whipped up war fever. The United States must save Cuba. *Cuba libre*: Free Cuba! The slogan spread over the United States.

On July 1, 1898, U.S. troops landed in Cuba. On July 17, the Spanish surrendered, and asked an ambassador in Washington to see about arranging peace terms. For some strange reason the ambassador was not able to get his message through right away. Indeed, it took four days. And during those four days, the U.S. General Nelson Miles sailed off to capture Puerto Rico with 3,415 men.

Most Puerto Ricans greeted the U.S. troops with enthusiasm. They had won freedom from Spain, and now the island would become part of the great American democracy.

"Oh, *si, si, si,*" said Muñoz Rivera to his son. "Was *mucho* wavings and kissings and cheerings for the soldiers of the U.S. as they march through the island. But I did not wave. No, I did not wave."

Muñoz Rivera looked at his son, and now there was no more laughter.

In the Treaty of Paris, as one of the spoils of war, Spain ceded Puerto Rico to the United States.*

For sixteen months the U.S. military ruled the island. Former Premier Muñoz Rivera went back to editing his newspaper. He spoke out so forcefully for the trampled rights of his people that he was thrown into jail to await trial. Prison was nothing new for him. He had been jailed by the Spanish forty-two times for speaking out against the government and for his people.

But this time, as he sat in the damp prison cell, he decided suddenly that he must move to the mainland. He must do what he could to let the American people know about the problems of *his* people. If they knew more about Puerto Rico perhaps they would care. And if they cared, perhaps they would help.

He had tried first as editor of the *Puerto Rico Herald*. But since that newspaper had been written for and read mainly by Puerto Ricans in New York City, it did little to affect the people who could help his island. The important people were the Congressmen and the President of the United States, who could pass legislation which would help his people to help themselves.

Which was why Luis Muñoz Rivera, the new resident commissioner, now sat on the leather-covered couch in his room in the Benedict Apartment Hotel, taking English conversation lessons from his thirteen-year-old son.

* The Treaty of Paris, which officially ended the Spanish-American War, was signed in Paris on December 10, 1898. The Philippines, as well as Puerto Rico, were ceded to the United States. Cuba was made a U.S. protectorate and became self-governing in 1902. The United States granted the Philippines independence on July 4, 1946.

CHAPTER 3

Within months father and son had grown so close that the resident commissioner moved his residence. The heavy leather-covered furniture, the old Victrola, the record collection and cartons of books were transported to the Highlands Apartment Hotel on Connecticut Avenue. Muñoz Rivera had taken an apartment with a large living room and two bedrooms—one of them for Luisito, who often stayed over on weekends.

As the years went by, father and son spent more and more time together. They were much alike. They were both poets. Indeed, Muñoz Rivera had been a published poet by the age of twenty-three. A newspaper editor named Ramon Marín bought his early poems. This same Marín had a beautiful daughter, Amalia. She sang minor roles at the Ponce Opera House. In 1893 Muñoz Rivera married Amalia Marín.

And now their only child, Luis Muñoz Marín, was writing poetry. "Like father, like son," Muñoz Rivera often said proudly. "Perhaps you will follow my footsteps into politics too."

Luisito always assured his father that he had no wish to become a politician. Yet, when he was graduated from Georgetown Prep at age sixteen, he followed his father's firm "suggestion" and went to Georgetown Law School at night. (Law, said Papá, was the best preparation for politics.)

Now Luisito lived, not in the dorms, but in his father's apartment. He would often come home late, around midnight. And the resident commissioner did not like that in the least. There were stern words, which were then undone when the two sat talking till four in the morning. They not only loved each other, but respected each other and enjoyed each other. And in those late-night "bull sessions" with his father, Luisito's education soared to new horizons.

Often in the daytime he brought his books to his father's office in Washington, D.C. He learned to type there, and he became the resident commissioner's very private secretary. Muñoz Rivera wrote out private political letters by hand on a yellow pad, and Luisito typed them and mailed them off on the ship which sailed once a week to Puerto Rico. In this way, and by overhearing conversations and arguments which went on in his father's office, Luisito learned more than he realized about the intricate inner workings of political life. He was receiving the finest education possible for a career he insisted he did not want.

There was another reason that Luisito liked to spend time in Muñoz Rivera's office: he had begun to worry about his papá's health. The resident commissioner began to lose weight. He sometimes seemed to be in pain.

Luisito begged his father to see a doctor. But Muñoz Rivera would merely laugh or shrug. "It's just something I ate," he would say. Or, "I'm tired. . . ." Or, "Who has the time for doctors?"

His father would sometimes agree to lie down to rest on the office couch, and then Luisito acted as a guardian, keeping all visitors away.

Finally, Muñoz Rivera said, "After my speech on the Jones Bill, then I will see a doctor. I promise you."

Luisito knew that his father was afraid to see a doctor, who might send him to a hospital or home to Puerto Rico before his most important mission was completed, the passage of the bill that would give Puerto Ricans a real say in the governing of their island.

Finally the day came—the day his father had been working for and living for ever since he arrived in Washington, D.C.

The resident commissioner of Puerto Rico was addressing the United States House of Representatives. Luisito had a front-row seat in the visitors' gallery. He sat tense, his eyes riveted on his father's face. He barely heard the words. He had no need to listen, for he knew the speech by heart. Muñoz Rivera had rehearsed it over and over, striding back and forth across the worn carpet of his room as Luisito, listened, corrected, and criticized the pronunciation. ("It is not *Ooo*manity, Papa. Say it again. *Hew*manity!")

As he listened to his father, Luisito fully realized how important those hours of English conversation had been. The illustrious Congressmen seated below were listening to the resident commissioner with real attention. And the words came across clear and strong—not hindered or half understandable because of poor pronunciation.

"Give us now the field of experiment which—which we ask of you, that we may—that we may show—"

Luisito leaned forward, fists clenched. His father had suddenly gone pale. Had the pain come back? *Please, God, let him get through this. Just this one more speech.*

It was a speech which could change the life of every man, woman, and child in Puerto Rico.

For the past sixteen years, ever since the U.S. military had been withdrawn as rulers in Puerto Rico, the island had lived under the rulings of the Foraker Act. The act provided for a Puerto Rican resident commissioner, who could sit in the House of Representatives, but who had no vote. The act also provided for a Puerto Rican House of Delegates in San Juan. They could vote on anything they liked. But it all meant nothing. For the American-appointed governor of the island could overrule whatever they decided. Only the American Congress could make laws for Puerto Rico. Furthermore, not only the governor, but the governor's Executive Committee, the commissioners of labor, education, health, agriculture—even the members of the Puerto Rican Supreme Court—were appointed by the President of the United States. And in most cases the President of the United States had never even been to Puerto Rico. In most cases he knew very little about the problems of the island.

Day after day, night after night, in meeting after meeting, with one official after another—including President Woodrow Wilson himself—Luis Muñoz Rivera had fought for a new bill. A bill which would give his people the right to rule themselves.

Luisito had sometimes gone with his father to these meetings. Muñoz Rivera always dressed carefully. If the cuffs of his white shirt were even slightly soiled, he would change the cuffs just before the meeting. He always took his cane, often wore his high silk hat. And as he appeared, so he spoke. Impressive. Dignified. Never pleading. Never demanding. Luisito always came away from the meeting certain that his papá was one of the greatest statesmen who had ever lived.

Muñoz Rivera was a practical man. He did not ask for the impossible. At this stage, he knew, the Americans would never give up their right to appoint the island's governor. He did not even ask as much as he had achieved long ago in his agreement with Sagasta of Spain.

He asked for the type of government England had granted Canada. And he sent a copy of that British agreement (Lord Durham's Report) together with his own typewritten letter to President Wilson, to every U.S. Congressman, to newsmen, to any official with any influence whatever on territorial matters. Why not, he asked, use the Lord Durham Report on Commonwealth or Dominion Status as a pattern for a new bill for Puerto Rico?

Representative William Jones from the state of Virginia was the man who listened most closely to the dedicated resident commissioner. And William Jones had finally introduced a bill which would mean a new lease on life for

Puerto Rico. It would give Puerto Ricans their own thirty-nine-man House of Representatives and nineteen-man Senate in San Juan. And what *these* men decided would mean something. If the American-selected governor vetoed one of their bills, they would have the right to go over his head—to the President of the United States.

But there was a gaping hole in *el Bill Jones,* as it was called on the island. Only Puerto Rican men who could read or write would be permitted to vote in island elections. And since less than 40 percent could read or write, this would mean that most Puerto Ricans would still have no say in their own government.

Muñoz Rivera was now requesting what seemed impossible. Even in the United States a person had to be able to read or write in order to vote.* But the resident commissioner was asking that the Jones Bill be amended to allow every Puerto Rican man the right to vote in island elections—whether or not he could read and write. This new ruling would mean that the voice of the *jíbaro* of the hills, the slum dweller of the cities—could at last be heard.

And these were the voices crying out to be heard.

These were the people ravaged by poverty and disease. These were the people who worked ten to twelve hours a day—when they were lucky—and received 40 cents to $1 a day for their labors. These were the people who lived in huts and hovels. These were the people dying in droves

* Although some states dropped the literacy requirement earlier, it was not until 1971 that literacy was dropped as a voting requirement for all voters in the United States.

from diphtheria, typhoid, tuberculosis; diseases with the death rate ever on the increase.

These were the people who had caused Puerto Rico to be called "the Cesspool of the Caribbean."

"Give us our independence and you will stand before humanity as the . . . as the greatest of the greats. . . ."

In anguish Luisito watched his father, who seemed to be aging before his eyes.

". . . a great creator of new nationalities and a great liberator of oppressed peoples."

It was over.

There was huge applause as the tall, dignified resident commissioner walked—very slowly—to his seat.

The House of Representatives passed the Jones Bill with some, but not all, of the changes which Muñoz Rivera had asked for. However, the voting amendment was there.

The Jones Bill was later passed by the Senate, signed by the President, and became law.

As well as granting Puerto Ricans more self-rule on the island itself, the Jones Bill decreed that, for the first time, Puerto Ricans would be full citizens of the United States. They could enter or leave the United States without passport or visa. They could, if they wished, move to any state in the Union without bothering about immigration papers or quotas. They would be protected by all U.S. laws, yet need not pay taxes to the federal government. And, for the first time, every male Puerto Rican on the island would have the right to vote for his own Senators and Representatives, who would meet in the gleaming white marble capitol building at the edge of Old San Juan.

In September, 1916, four months after he had made his famous speech on "*el Bill Jones,*" Luis Muñoz Rivera left Washington. He was going home.

"I'm tired, that's all," he told his son. "I need a good rest. You stay here. Finish your studies at Georgetown. I'll return soon."

"No, Papá," Luisito said firmly. "I am coming with you."

His father exploded. Luisito must not interrupt his law school career. For what? There was no reason. But the words trailed off as Muñoz Rivera was racked with violent pain.

The doctor told Luisito that his father had cancer of the liver; there was no hope. It would be a matter of months, that was all.

They took the boat home together.

At first they went, on the insistence of Muñoz Rivera, to a small farm he owned in Santurce, in the suburbs of San Juan. "Fresh air, sunlight, quiet; that's all I need," he insisted.

But it soon was clear that he needed much more.

He was moved to the palatial home of Eduardo Georgetti, one of the richest men on the island and a close friend and admirer of Luis Muñoz Rivera. There he received the finest possible medical attention. But it was much too late.

On November 15, 1916, Muñoz Rivera died at the age of

fifty-nine.

His funeral was the longest and most memorable in the island's four centuries of recorded history.

It was a fitting end for the man they called "the George Washington of Puerto Rico."

Although no one realized it at the time—including Luisito himself—the funeral was an important beginning for Luis Muñoz Rivera's son and heir.

CHAPTER 4

The coffin was placed in the back of a large black Pierce-Arrow, the finest car in the island. It belonged to Georgetti. And the cortege started at Georgetti's home, where Muñoz Rivera died. It would end in the mountain-top town of Barranquitas, the great man's birthplace.

But the body of *El León* would not be taken directly to Barranquitas. All the island mourned for the dead hero. All the islanders must be permitted their last farewell.

The Pierce-Arrow drove first through the streets of San Juan. It was a splendid sunny day and an enormous throng massed in the streets. There were so many flowers that the procession seemed like a walking flower garden.

Behind the Pierce-Arrow came another car, carrying Luisito and his mother; behind them a dozen more cars; and behind them horses and carriages, men on horseback. *Jíbaros,* the poverty-ridden people of the hills, rode on burros, and thousands of men and women walked behind, weeping.

The procession moved through the capital city and into the countryside. Sometimes it was large; sometimes it dwindled. But always there were people who lined the roads. "Muñoz," they cried. "Muñoz, our father!"

Many knelt and prayed as the procession went by. Some who came in the nighttime carried candles. Luisito could see their tears by the tiny glimmering candlelight.

It was a strange, sad way to tour the country. But during that funeral procession Luisito came to know his island as he never had before.

He saw the gangs of ragged homeless children begging in the towns, picking fruit from trees in the countryside in order to stay alive. In the town of San Germán he was told that children roosted in the trees at night. They had no other place to sleep.

Few of the *jíbaros* he spoke to knew how to read or write. The full importance of his father's last speech came home to him. Under the Jones Bill these men would be able to vote for the betterment of their lives.

Some of the men, women, and children who lined the roads wore white rags around their heads. When Luisito asked why, he was told the people believed the white cloths would cure their diseases. Perhaps they needed a belief such as this. They had nothing else. There were not many doctors on the island, and almost none who tended the *jíbaro*.

Ninety percent of the country people were infected with hookworm, a disease which drained them of energy and which sometimes caused death. In the towns and cities the poor were afflicted by sprue, a type of dysentery which also often caused death. And spreading all over the island was the dread disease tuberculosis—TB. The missionaries had renamed it "tinbox," for many of the houses were roofed with corrugated zinc, sided with sheet iron from old gasoline cans. At night the countrymen closed every window tight, believing the night air to be harmful. The sweltering moist nights inside the over-crowded "tin boxes" turned these island homes into breeding grounds for TB.

More fortunate, from this standpoint, were those who still lived in the old-fashioned thatched huts. But these wooden shacks often slid down the mountainside after a heavy rain.

And over half the land was mountains and hills. As the funeral procession chugged up the steep roads or wended its slow way down hairpin, cliff-lined curves, Luisito was reminded of the schoolbook story he had read as a child. When Columbus was asked by Queen Isabella what the island looked like, he crumpled up a sheet of paper, tossed it onto the table before her, and said, "It looks like *that,* Your Majesty."

It was a small island, about 100 miles long and 35 miles wide, which was why this idea of *El León's* farewell trip was not an impossible one. In a few days one could, in fact, cover the main passable roads. And there were many roads. The old ones had been built by the Spaniards; the new by the Americans—under pressure from the sugar barons. For sugar was the island's main industry. Sugar, once grown only on the coastal plains, and which needed roads to be trucked to the ports, had now invaded the mountain slopes. Sugar, which was shipped to the main-land to make a handful of men millionaire-wealthy. Sugar, which kept most of the islanders starvation-poor. The *jíbaros* who worked on the sugar plantations earned about a dollar a day, which was not bad as Puerto Rican wages went. However, the work season lasted only five months. The remaining months were called the "dead season." It was well named, for during these dreaded months the *jíbaros* did, indeed, have trouble remaining alive. Of all the diseases which afflicted the population, unemployment was perhaps the worst one of all.

Yet, despite their hardships, the hill people were kind, gentle, and courteous. Luisito met many of them when—as often happened—the cars of the funeral procession were stuck in the mud. Then, from nowhere it seemed, men would appear to strain and struggle and move the heavy automobiles with their own strength, sometimes shoving them halfway up a mountain road. At such times Luisito got out to help. And, shoulder to shoulder with a *jíbaro,* he learned a good deal about his countrymen. Often he did not return to the car, but walked on for a while, talking to these men of the hills, growing close to them.

On the day the funeral procession reached Barranquitas, over 30,000 people came to pay their final respects. It was the largest crowd ever to have gathered in a Puerto Rican town.

As the body of their hero was lowered into the ground, they pressed around the grave site. Wealthy, well-dressed gentlemen from the city and barefoot *jíbaros* in clean-washed white cotton trousers and shirts. They removed their *pavas*—straw hats—from their heads as the ritual words of the priest rose into the air. There were crippled beggars who had somehow climbed up the endless mountain road to Barranquitas, one of the highest towns on the island. And there were thousands of women—city women in the stylish dresses fashionable on the mainland and country women of the hills, many of them almost in rags, but wearing elegant lace shawls which they had made themselves. (The hill women were famed for their fine needlework, for which they earned—if they were lucky—a few cents an hour.)

Luisito fully realized that it was not only *his* father whose body was being lowered into the ground. Luis Muñoz Rivera was a father figure to each of them. Now they were alone, as he was. Now they felt lost, as he did.

The words of the priest were submerged by the sound of people sobbing.

The funeral was over. The thousands of mourners would now return to their homes. But the tropical night had come on swiftly. The way down the dark mountain road was a long one. And people were hungry. They wanted something to eat before setting out.

Within a half hour after the funeral the few stores in Barranquitas had been sold out. There was nothing left on the shelves. So the people of Barranquitas opened the doors of their homes and shared everything they had with these strangers, who were, somehow, suddenly brothers, bound close by grief. And those who had brought baskets of food for the trip home shared what they had with others who were equally hungry but had nothing.

The simple giving spirit of Luis Muñoz Rivera was close to the people in Barranquitas that night.

Several days later, as he wandered alone along the Barranquitas road, Luisito felt a poem forming in his mind—a poem, a cry, a confession.

He was the only child of a dead hero. But he was not able to follow in his father's footsteps.

He recited the words softly—

If I were only a giant
to embrace these mountains that he contemplated in his boyhood,
the mountains for which he struggled from his youth onward,
the mountains that shelter his countrymen, the *jíbaros* . . .
and now entomb his body. . . .
If I were only a giant
to hold close all these Puerto Ricans
who keep forever in their hearts the sacred memory of my father.
If I were only a giant . . .
to complete the work of Luis Muñoz Rivera. . . .*

But Luisito was no giant. Indeed, he had never felt so small as he wondered down the mountain road, alone.

* Translated by Marianne Norris in her book, *Father and Son for Freedom,* Dodd, Mead & Co., New York, 1968.

CHAPTER 5

Luis Muñoz Rivera left everything he had to his wife and his son. When the provisions of the will were published, Puerto Ricans were stunned. They had known Don Luis was an honest man. But for years he had been the most important and powerful man on the island. His friends and loyal followers included millionaire sugar barons like Georgetti. People assumed that the dignified, impressive-looking, well-dressed resident commissioner must, of course, be wealthy. He certainly had . . . opportunities!

But he left only $400.

Doña Amalia was running a boardinghouse in New York City. The friends of Muñoz Rivera felt that this was not a fitting career for the widow of their most eminent and beloved citizen. They raised money and bought the house on Fortaleza Street in Old San Juan where the newspaper *La Democracia* had its offices. This they presented to Doña Amalia. She could live upstairs and rent the ground floors to the newspaper, which would bring her a small monthly income.

As for Luisito, the $200 his father had left him would not go very far. It was obvious that he would have to go to work. But at what? And where? And for whom?

There were many pressures on him. His mother wanted him to go back to law school, work his way through.

Friends of his father wanted him to remain on the island, involve himself in politics, prepare himself for the giant task of stepping into his father's footsteps. But this, Luisito declared, he had no intention of doing. Just because he bore his father's name did not mean he should be expected to sink himself in the mire of Puerto Rican problems and politics.

He was eighteen years old. He was free of the demanding pressures and worrries which the last few years with Muñoz Rivera had meant. And he intended to *be* free—to live his life as *he* wanted it.

He made two special friends: de Diego Padró and Luis Pales Matos. They were young poets. And, with Luisito, they became the Three Musketeers. They spent their days lolling on a sunny beach, swimming, picnicking, drinking *cerveza* and reciting poetry—theirs and others. Standing barefoot on the beach, with the ocean as his backdrop, Luisito—tall, suntanned, and handsome—would translate with fervor the works of his favorite North American poets: Robert Frost, Vachel Lindsay, Walt Whitman and, above all, Edwin Markham. And his companions listened, enthralled.

In the evenings they returned to Old San Juan and made for their favorite restaurant, La Mallorquina, which had been a headquarters for artists, writers, and politicians since it was founded in 1848. The front of the restaurant opened onto the street, and the young men had a favorite table there by the wrought-iron fence where they sat watching the world go by and making their colorful comments about it.

Or sometimes they sat by the stained glass windows overlooking the back patio, and as the overhead fan stirred the warm, heavy air they would write down the words they had composed in the daytime.

When La Mallorquina closed in the early hours of the morning, the three young men would wander through the quiet streets of Old San Juan, still sounding off loudly on politics, poetry, and people.

"That one is the son of *El León*," people would say in dismay. To carry the renowned name of Muñoz and sink down the drain!

But Luisito was not sinking.

In 1917, at the age of nineteen, he held his first published book in his hands. It was called *Borrones (Ink Blots)*. It included a one-act play which had been "produced many times in the theatre of my dreams with great success." The book also included fantasy and essays, serious and humorous. And it included a prologue written by one of Puerto Rico's most famous poets, who noted in kindly tones that Muñoz Marín showed some promise as a writer and then launched into three pages of praise about the great Luis Muñoz Rivera, whose "death closed what we may call our Puerto Rican heroic period. It is gone forever."

Soon Luisito's slender inheritance ran out. And he

found that he could no longer tolerate living in the shadow of his dead father. Late in 1917 he applied for a job as secretary to the new resident commissioner, Feliz Córdova Dávila. This was one job for which the young man ideally qualified. His typing was good. His English was perfect. And, most important, he knew his way around Washington.

The "Muñoz-watchers" breathed in relief. Luisito was back on the track; he was on the way.

He not only worked for the commissioner, but gathered up the many important poems, essays, and political papers which his father had never published and prepared them for publication.* And he wrote his own essays, articles, and poems for the newspaper his father had founded, *La Democracia*.

Suddenly after fourteen months Luisito quit his job, left Washington, and returned to Puerto Rico to raise funds for a new Spanish-English journal which he planned to publish in the United States. He traveled around the island for three months. He did not raise much money, but he did raise more looming comparisons with his father. Comparisons and expectations. His father's followers urged that he go into politics. There were many political parties in Puerto Rico. And Luisito did attend some meetings. Crowds would whisper when he walked in; they stared at him. Sometimes there was even a shout: "Long live the son of Muñoz Rivera!"

* Luis Muñoz Rivera's collected works were published in 1924.

Although Luisito had grown very close to his father during the Washington years, he was now beginning to feel deep resentments, anger. Why could they not see him as he was: Luis Muñoz Marín—a young man of twenty who wanted to found and edit a new publication to be called *La Revista de Indias (The Review of the Indies)*? Why did he have to be seen always as his father's son? Even in private gatherings he stopped referring to "Papá" or "my father." It was now always "Muñoz Rivera"—a distant figure. He was shoving off the smothering shadow, or trying to. But they would not let him. So finally he fled.

Not to Washington, this time, but to the place of his happiest boyhood memories; the place where they had lived as a family: Mamá, Papá, and Luisito. Manhattan.

But he did not go back to the Upper West Side. He went instead to that part of Manhattan which was a beacon and a magnet for young poets, writers, editors, artists, and intellectuals throughout the United States: Greenwich Village.

He rented a one-room walkup. He took an extension course in playwriting at Columbia University. He worked on his new magazine, *The Review of the Indies*. The first issue was published in September, 1918. Late at night, he wrote poetry. It was published not only in *La Democracia,* but also in newspapers and magazines in Buenos Aires, Panama, and Cuba. And another book was published: *Madre Haraposa (Mother in Rags)*. The by-line: Luis Muñoz Marín.

Luisito was succeeding—on his own—in the field he loved most: writing.

And somehow, in between the work-crammed hours, he had time for friends and parties. One night, at one of these parties, he met an American girl from Mississippi. She was gentle, soft-spoken, and attractive. She had a round face, dark eyes, dark-brown hair, and pale skin. She wore no makeup. There was an uncombed, uncared-for look about her which Luisito found appealing. (He had, in fact, the same look himself.)

In any case, Miss Muna Lee, from Mississippi, obviously had more on her mind than what she wore and how she looked.

They sat in a corner on a broken-down couch, talking. She too was a poet; indeed, at twenty-four Muna had already made something of a reputation for herself—not only as a poet, but also as a translator (her Spanish was perfect) and as a critic of Spanish and Latin American literature. Furthermore, as Muñoz was amused to learn, shy-seeming, soft-spoken Muna Lee was a leader in the feminist movement.

She was obviously fascinated by the impassioned, poetic, charming, and outgoing Luisito. When he suggested that she come to work on his new literary journal, she agreed at once. The salary he offered was small. But it was not the salary which interested her.

On July 1, 1919, Muna Lee and Luis Muñoz were married.

Suddenly life expanded for Luisito. It was like living one of his own daydreams.

CHAPTER 6

Muna and Muñoz.

Their names became a byword among the young intellectuals in Greenwich Village. Their Sunday-evening at-homes were a highlight of Village life.

Every Sunday evening their small apartment was crowded with a fascinating collection of men and women; some famous, some unknown. But each was special in his or her own way. Among the famous were the American poets Archibald MacLeish, Carl Sandburg, Sara Teasdale, Vachel Lindsay, and William Rose Benét. And Edwin Markham.

Only three years previously, when he had stood on the beach reciting Markham's poems to the other Musketeers, Luisito scarcely dreamed that the great man would one day take the slow ferry trip from Staten Island, followed by a subway ride, in order to be present at a party given by Luisito Muñoz Marín.

There were always Puerto Ricans at the party, and Latin Americans: journalists, poets, and political exiles. The Spanish bullfighter Belmonte showed up for the Sunday at-homes whenever he was in New York. And there were "regulars" from far-off places, whom Muñoz found particularly intriguing: such as the famed Arctic explorers Vilhjalmur Stefansson and Hubert Wilkins. As a man from an island which had no winter, Luisito was enthralled by stories of these lands where it was winter most of the time.

In addition to their explosively exciting social life, the young couple were forging ahead impressively in their careers. They had very little money—which did not bother them in the least. What did matter was that Muna was winning prizes for her poetry. And Luisito's poems were beginning to appear in the showplace for important poets: *Poetry Magazine*. In addition, he wrote articles and essays for three of the nation's most highly respected magazines: *Smart Set, The American Mercury*, and *The Nation*. And his own magazine—with Muna and Muñoz as chief editors and contributors—was beginning to make itself felt as a force in the Spanish-American literary and political world.

Perhaps the best part about it all was the fact that, by age twenty-two, Luisito had made it on his own. This world of his dreams which he lived every day had nothing whatever to do with the fact that he was the son of the great Don Luis. Most of the people he met in New York had forgotten his father's name. Some of them had never even heard of Muñoz Rivera.

But in Puerto Rico, Luis Muñoz Rivera was far from forgotten. And there were many who were waiting for his son to come back home.

Antonio Barceló was the most fervent of these men. He was editor of *La Democracia* and head of the Partido

Unión de Puerto Rico, which Muñoz Rivera had helped to found. "Come back," Barceló kept writing to Luisito. "We need a Muñoz. We need you *here!*"

Luisito tried to disregard the letters. He was torn. The life he loved—and which he had created for himself—was in Manhattan. He knew full well what awaited him at home: political conflicts and a whole cesspool of insoluble problems. He knew the statistics; he had written about them.

Puerto Rico had the highest infant mortality in the world.

In some villages 100 percent of the people had malaria.

The average wage of the jíbaro was $100 a year.

Americans averaged three-quarters of a pint of milk a day. Puerto Ricans averaged a teaspoon a day, milk that was unpasteurized and usually unfit to drink.

The population density on the island was one of the highest in the world.

In any direction one chose to look—health, education, income, labor conditions, unemployment—the problems of Puerto Rico were dismal and seemed insurmountable. The author John Gunther wrote that the villages he had seen in Puerto Rico were filthier, more squalid, and more disease-ridden than any he had seen in the worst parts of India or China.

Luisito wrote back to Barceló: "I can do more here to help, with my articles. I can stir up public opinion."

Barceló replied that this argument was only an excuse. He begged Muñoz to come home and campaign for the

Partido Unión de Puerto Rico in the 1920 elections. ''We need you to help us win,'' he wrote. ''Then, if you must, return to the Mainland.''

Muñoz's mother, Doña Amalia, added her voice to Barceló's pleas.

Finally Luisito wrote back: ''Muna is pregnant. After the baby arrives—I will come for the election campaign.''

The baby girl was born in the winter of 1920. They named her after her mother, and called her Munita.

Muñoz had never thought very much about being a father. But now that he was one, his tiny baby daughter seemed the most incredible thing in the world. He adored the baby. And he wished back the promise he had made to Barceló and his mother.

Nevertheless, he had made a promise. And in March, 1920, he took the steamer to Puerto Rico. The elections were in November. But he had no intention of remaining away from Muna, Munita, and Manhattan for that long. He would do what he could to help Barceló. He would gather information for more articles on the problems of Puerto Rico. Then he would return to the Mainland; he would come back home.

But things did not work out the way he had planned. He moved into his mother's apartment on the third floor of the old house on San Francisco Street. The offices of *La Democracia* were downstairs. It seemed the obvious place for him to stay. He loved being with his wise and witty mother. And he was on hand for conferences with Barceló and other *Unionistas,* conferences which could come at any time of the day or the night, and which always seemed to go on for hours.

But the more Luisito heard at these meetings of the top party leaders, the more he wished that he had taken a place of his own, where he could be free—free to go out and meet the people and free to meet the leaders of other political parties.

It seemed all too evident to the young man that his father's party had changed since the days when it was led by *El León*. Muñoz Rivera had cared about the "common man"—the *jíbaro* of the hills and the slum dweller of the towns and cities. He had also been, as he termed it, a *posibilista*—a realist who aimed for ends which were possible under the circumstances.

But it seemed to Luisito that the party leaders had become 100 percent *posibilitas,* and this meant—in their view—cooperating, for the present, with the wealthy American and Puerto Rican sugar barons who ran the island. Idealism was set aside if its ends were not "possible" in the next election. First things first, they said. We must win the election. Then we can look out for the lot of the common man.

Luisito realized that this approach was sound and sensible. But was it sincere? If the *Unionistas* won the election, would the party leaders suddenly turn their backs on powerful and wealthy friends in order to help the people for whom the party had been founded?

There was one party in Puerto Rico—and only one—which was speaking out strongly for the principles in which Luis Muñoz Marín believed: the Socialists.

In New York City he had spent many inspiring hours talking about Socialism with Edwin Markham and others whom he admired. They were members of the Socialist Party in the United States. He was stirred by their sincerity; by their concepts of liberty, equality, fraternity; by their dedication to bettering the lot of the common man—"The Man with the Hoe," Markham called him. A man who had "The emptiness of ages in his face, And on his back the burdens of the world. . . ."

In Puerto Rico the head of the Socialist Party, Santiago Iglesias, was speaking out with eloquence for "The Man with the Hoe." So dedicated was Iglesias to the ideals of liberty, equality, and fraternity that he had named three of his daughters Libertad, Igualdad, and Fraternidad.

But Santiago Iglesias and Muñoz Rivera had been enemies. Muñoz Rivera had once had Iglesias arrested. And once, in La Mallorquina, Muñoz Rivera had become so angry while arguing with Iglesias that he threw his cane at the man. He missed. But the cane broke the rim of a huge blue Mallorcan urn which stood near their table. During the carefree days, Luisito and his Musketeers had looked at this urn and laughed about it.

But now, in the year 1920, there was no laughter in Luisito. He was torn; all ways. He missed his wife. Since their marriage a year previously, Muna had shared in his work and his life in every way. Now, with the baby to bind them, they were closer than ever. He missed his baby daughter to a degree which astounded him. How could she have come to mean so much to him in a few months' time?

And Luisito was torn, politically.

How could he go out and speak for the *Unionistas* when he disagreed with so much of what their present leaders stood for? On the other hand, how could he campaign for the Socialists and thereby take a public stand against his father's party and his father's most loyal friends and followers? Besides, the Socialist Party of Puerto Rico was new. It had figured in only one islandwide election, and of the 175,000 votes cast, the Socialists had pulled only 24,468. What use to risk everything in speaking out for a party and a cause which could not possibly win?

Luisito resolved his problems—or tried to—by escaping from them.

In the early morning hours he would stagger home drunk through the streets, the blue-brick streets of Old San Juan, which the Three Muskeeteers had once jauntily called their Blue-Brick Kingdom. Had that been only four years ago? It seemed another lifetime away; a carefree lifetime.

Sometimes when he did not come home, Doña Amalia asked Barceló to look for her son. And Barceló often found him in a speakeasy, too drunk to get home.

Barceló was a vibrant, well-meaning, and emotional man, "Please, Luisito," he would plead. "What are you doing to yourself? To us? We need you."

And the son of Muñoz Rivera would shout, "You don't need *me*! You need a Muñoz. You need my name, that's all—my father's name!"

As he helped the young man to his feet, Barceló would often say gently, "Come, Luisito, we'll get you home."

Once, the young man looked at his father's friend and said. "Home? Barceló, my home is sixteen hundred miles away in Manhattan. Here on the island, Barceló, I have no home."

CHAPTER 7

In May Luisito told his mother that he planned to join the Puerto Rican Socialist Party.

Doña Amalia stared at her son and then announced: "You must be drunk."

"I am perfectly sober," said Luisito.

Doña Amalia was a strong-willed woman, fiery, demanding. It was one reason she and her husband had separated. There were too many arguments. She never gave in easily. She liked the sparks to fly.

And she did not give in now. "It is because of your father!" she shouted. "You were always jealous of his position. Now—after he is in the grave four years—you find this way to kick him, to spit on his memory."

"No, Mamá," Luisito said wearily. "If it had not been for Papá and what he means to me, I would have come out for the Socialists two months ago. Now I must catch up for lost time. I will do everything I can to help Iglesias."

"Help Iglesias?" his mother shrieked. "*Help* him? Nothing can help him. He has to lose. You know that. Everyone knows that!"

Then Luisito quoted something he once had written: "We learn by planting things in the mind that later bear fruit in understanding."

"You are a madman," his mother announced.

"The Socialists cannot win in November, 1920," Luisito said. "But if their message is heard and understood by enough people, perhaps someday—"

Suddenly Doña Amalia shouted, "I have a weak heart! If you become a Socialist, I may have a heart attack. I may die."

"This is the first I have heard of your weak heart, Mamá," said Luisito. "You have always been as strong as a horse."

"A horse can have a weak heart," Doña Amalia pointed out. "But—" She shrugged. "If you want to kill me, go ahead. Join Iglesias, Become a Socialist."

"Since I plan to stay till November," said Luisito, "I have asked Muna to bring the baby and join me here. The question is, do you want a Socialist in your house? Or shall I look for some other place to live?"

After a long moment Doña Amalia said, "I invite my little granddaughter to live with me. If her parents wish to join her here, that is up to them."

"Thank you, Mamá." Luisito kissed her.

But she shoved him away. "I don't want to be there when you tell Barceló," she said. And she spat the word after him: *"Socialist!"*

When Barceló learned that the son of his friend and idol was campaigning for the Socialist Party he ordered that the name Luis Muñoz Marín should never be mentioned in *La Democracia*, no matter how much "news" the young man might make.

And Luisito did make news. He developed a new method of political campaigning.

In his first speech before a large crowd he extolled with drama and poetry the marvelous beauties of Puerto Rico, the azure sky, the glorious Caribbean sea, the sweep of sandy beaches. And at the end of each dramatic paragraph, he paused so that the crowd could roar approval. This was the way all politicians campaigned in Puerto Rico—with florid platitudes. And the people knew their "part": when to clap and chant and cheer.

Suddenly, however, Muñoz stopped. He looked at his listeners and asked, "Why do you applaud me? I have not said anything." Whereupon he launched into a dire but realistic description of the misery of the destitute workers and their exploitation by the sugar magnates. This time there was no applause at all. But the crowd listened with deep attention. And in that single speech Muñoz started the beginning of the end of florid, inane political speeches in Puerto Rico.

Furthermore, Muñoz, as he put it, "refused the dictatorship of the horse." Other politicians would come galloping into a village where a speech had been scheduled. They would make their speech—to great applause—then jump on their horse and trot away.

But Luis Muñoz Marín walked.

He would enter a town on foot, stroll through the streets, sit on a bench in the plaza, and talk to people. He would hear not only their complaints, but their ideas. Each of the speeches he gave was directly related to the people in *that* town or village. And when he walked on after the speech, he was often accompanied for miles by villagers and *jíbaros* who asked his advice and his help.

He learned then the tragic outcome of all the fighting his father had done so that illiterate men in Puerto Rico would vote. Yes, according to the Jones Bill they could vote. And they much appreciated this right—for a man could sell his vote to a wealthy sugar baron. A vote was worth $2, which represented a new pair of shoes or a bottle of rum! Not only were live votes sold, but votes of the dead were worth money, too. Muñoz heard the story of a carload of political workers who passed a cemetery in the evening. They had some undistributed handbills, which they merrily tossed over the wall onto the gravestones. When one of the workers pointed out that the handbills cost money and should not be wasted, he was told, "Wasted? Those fellows vote too, don't they?"

In speech after speech Muñoz begged the people of the hills and the villages not to sell their votes. They were giving away their only chance to fight for a better life for themselves. But, whereas other points he made always raised cheers of enthusiasm, the people turned cold on this one. He spoke, but they did not hear. And, as he looked at the squalor in which they lived, it was easy enough for Luisito to understand why $2 in the pocket meant more than a packet of future hopes and promises.

Luisito proved to be a powerful speaker; far better than

his father had been. Don Luis was an imposing man, always well dressed. Even when campaigning in the hills, he would change his well-starched shirt cuffs if they seemed wilted. He spoke in short sentences, cut and dried, to the point. His voice, too, was cut and dried. He could move people as a writer more effectively than as an orator.

But his son excelled in both. He had a strong baritone voice and a way with words which could stir his listeners to frenzies of enthusiasm. They liked the way he looked and dressed. Rumpled hair, rumpled shirt hanging over khaki trousers. Even when addressing a hall filled with city dwellers, he never wore a tie. He was not above them, they felt. He was of them.

His sincerity was obvious, especially since he was not even running for office himself. He was the biggest drawing card the Socialist Party had. Other parties put out rumors about him, hoping to stem his popularity: the son of the revered Muñoz Rivera was a drunk, a dope addict. He lived a wild life in New York City.

But the people paid no attention. They would sometimes walk all night if they knew that the son of the great Don Luis was to speak at a nearby village the next day.

Luis began to wonder why they came. Was it to see the only son of their dead hero? Or was it to hear what he, Luis Muñoz Marín, had to say?

He tried an experiment. He was scheduled to make an important speech in Ponce, Puerto Rico's third-largest city. But he forbade any mention of his father's name in the advance publicity. When he spoke in Ponce, the hall was almost empty.

There had perhaps been a grain of truth in his mother's accusation. Perhaps he had joined the Socialist Party in part to fight his way free from his father's shadow. He thought he was succeeding—until he stared out bitterly at the empty seats in the Ponce auditorium.

Well, when the election was over, he would return home to Manhattan, where he was known and respected as Luis Muñoz Marín!

The Socialists did badly in the election, as had been expected. Yet they pulled twice as many votes as they had the first time.

Iglesias persuaded Luisito to stay on, for a few months at least. They needed him—as a writer, a speechmaker, and organizer, and—yes, as the son and symbol of the greatest hero Puerto Rico ever had.

Muna was pregnant again. And Muñoz promised Iglesias that he would stay in Puerto Rico until after the baby was born.

On August 1, 1921, the tiny black-haired Luis Muñoz Lee lay gurgling in his bassinet. As the father looked at his day-old son he wondered whether *his* papá had felt this fusion of pride, tenderness, and love when he saw his son for the first time.

Some months later, five members of the Muñoz family left for Manhattan. Doña Amalia was so much in love with her two small grandchildren that she declared she could not live without them and would henceforth live with them.

As he stood on the deck of the steamer, watching the city of San Juan recede into the distance, Luisito was overcome by a wrenching sadness. Was he going home?

Or was he leaving home? Where *were* his roots—on the island or the Mainland? Roots were made in childhood. As a child he had spent most of his years on the Mainland. Yet, in the past months, traveling to all corners of the island, he had made new roots; strong ones.

Was he a writer or a politician? Which way could he help his people most? He loved writing. Politics was a harsh and a heartbreaking world. (Look what he had done to his father's loyal disciple, Barceló.) His father had tried first as an editor and writer in Manhattan, and had then realized that, despite all its drawbacks, politics offered the most effective way. Was he, Luisito, running out? Running away?

Muna came up on deck and stood beside him. "We've imported a fine baby-sitter," she told him. "It's not all children who have an opera-singing grandma to lullaby them to sleep."

He put his arm around her and turned away from the distant island to look at the empty sun-sparked ocean which stretched ahead to the sky.

CHAPTER 8

The conflict stayed with him for ten years.

He wrote about Puerto Rico. And what he said was effective.

On January 4, 1922, he published an article in *The New Republic*. Its title: "A 98 Percent American in Puerto Rico." Its subject: the hated all-American governor of the island, E. Montgomery Reilly, who seemed to feel that he had been given a mandate to make the sugar barons richer still, while allowing the people of Puerto Rico to sink deeper into the mire of poverty and hopelessness.

Muñoz's article revealed so many shocking details about Reilly's "reign" that the piece was widely discussed in Washington circles. President Harding asked for Reilly's resignation. And many believed that the Reilly-blasting article by Muñoz had been, in large measure, responsible for the ousting of the governor.

There were other important pieces which helped make people aware of conditions in "Puerto Rico: The American Colony" (as a Muñoz article in *The Nation* was called).

Largely because of the eloquent pen of Luis Muñoz Marín, the plight of Puerto Rico was kept before the American public, exposed like a gaping wound. But what was achieved by exposure? What was being done to heal the wounds? Very little.

Was politics the way?

Suddenly the Socialist Santiago Iglesias did an abrupt about-face. His party of the workers joined forces with the Republican Party in Puerto Rico—the party of the wealthy landowners, who wore the boots which kept the poor trodden down in the dirt. The Republicans now touted Iglesias as a distinguished gentleman, and he was elected as resident commissioner. He came to Washington, D.C., with his three daughters in tow.

"Libertad, Igualidad, and Fraternidad!" Muñoz scoffed. "He should change their names now!"

Barceló began writing once again to Luisito. "Come back. We need you."

And, on June 14, 1926, the family did return—but only, Luisito made clear, because of *La Democracia*. The paper was failing. Since his mother's slender income was tied to that of the newspaper, he had come back to see if he could help boost the circulation. That was all.

Within ten days he had taken over as editor-in-chief of the newspaper—to Barceló's delight and to Luisito's dismay. Not only were there barely enough subscribers to keep the paper alive, but the plant and the printing press were falling to pieces. Muñoz slaved over his first editorial—one which, he hoped, would bring back some of the old readers. But the typesetter sent back his piece. "Our *f*'s are all worn out," he said. "You'll have to rewrite this editorial so it has no letter *f*'s in it."

In New York the struggle for money had been a constant one. They had moved to Riverside Drive and then to New Jersey in an attempt to find more rooms for less rent. Since Muna was not one for making fancy meals or for wearing fancy clothes, they managed to squeeze by on the checks which came in from their writing—$25 here; $15 there.

But in Puerto Rico the little money they had went to buy new *f*'s for the newspaper and for other such essentials. The children had no meat or milk. So one day Muna went off to the University of Puerto Rico and came back with a double job. She would teach American poetry and she would be publicity director of the university.

Muna loved her new life and was quite content to stay in Puerto Rico forever.

But when the struggling paper was back on its feet again, Luisito announced that they were returning to the Mainland.

Barceló was stunned. He had founded a new Liberal Party. But he was an old man now. He saw Luisito as his political heir.

And Muna was stunned. "Why?" she asked. "Just when everything's beginning to go well here, why leave?"

Muñoz could not answer her. He had asked the same question of himself. There was no answer.

On the day he had arrived back on the island he had been interviewed on his future plans. The article ran on the front page of *El Mundo*. "I bide my time," he had said, "in politics and in literature."

He was still biding his time, waiting—for what?

Back in the United States he continued writing important articles about Puerto Rico. But sometimes he would simply disappear from the scene. He would take off in his old car and drive wherever his whim suggested. If he had a little money in his pockets, he would sleep in a run-down hotel. If there was no money, he slept in the car. He had a weekly assignment from the Baltimore *Sun,* and he did an occasional article for the New York *Herald Tribune*. This provided enough money for gas and for the hamburgers and bananas on which he lived.

Muna's university paychecks and Doña Amalia's rent money from *La Democracia* supported the children during these periods.

It was Muna who begged him now: *Come home to us. The children need you. I need you. What are you doing? What are you searching for?*

What could he tell her? He did not know.

The winter of 1930–1931 was shot through with freezing days and nights.

The Great Depression had descended upon the United States, and no one wanted to read articles about the plight of Puerto Ricans. Muñoz took to ghost-writing articles signed by other men. But he could not make enough money to pay for even the cheapest hotel room. He slept in the car and shivered through the long nights.

Finally, the writer Lewis Gannett offered Luisito the

use of his country house in Connecticut. And Muñoz stayed there alone for the rest of the winter, chopping his own firewood and living on the canned food he had brought with him.

When the warm weather came, Luis Muñoz Marín got into his rattling old car and drove to New York City. He looked up an old friend of Muna's, gave her the car, walked down to the docks, and boarded a steamer for Puerto Rico.

He was going home.

CHAPTER 9

Whatever Muñoz had been searching for during those long-lost months, it was clear to everyone that he had found it. He had found himself.

He and his family settled in and settled down on the second floor of the house owned by Doña Amalia at 92 San Francisco Street. Muñoz did not have far to travel to work in the mornings. Barceló gave him back his old job as editor of *La Democracia* for $23 a week. But since the printing press and other offices took up all of the first floor, Muñoz made his office in a spacious room on the second floor, which opened onto the long wrought-iron balcony. There were three small rooms behind this office, the family bedrooms—sparsely furnished—and the kitchen.

Doña Amalia had a new story built for herself, and she lived here alone on the third floor. She guarded her privacy carefully.

Muñoz plunged at once into the complications of island politics, and meetings were held in his office, day and night. But if any of the enthusiastic politicians tried to visit Doña Amalia in her realm, she would block their way with the announcement: "The revolution stops at the second floor!"

The second-floor politicians were not envisioning a revolution—though the continual shouting and arguing often sounded as though one were brewing.

Muñoz had agreed to work for Barceló's new Liberal Party. But his followers and Barceló's differed on one plank in the party platform which each regarded as all-important.

Muñoz and his men—most of them young, vital, vibrant—felt that the Liberal Party should favor independence for Puerto Rico. The distinguished-looking Barceló, with his shock of wavy gray hair and dignified manner, led the more experienced and elderly faction. They felt that Puerto Rico would fare best in the long run by aiming for statehood rather than cutting itself off from the United States.

Muñoz saw the goal of independence as a way of breaking free of the terrible lethargy and despondency which seemed to have settled down like a physical force, blanketing the island. "I want my people to want independence!" he shouted at one of the late-night meetings. "Once they do want it, they will begin to struggle for the improvement of their own lives."

Because the old-line Liberal Party members needed the surging vitality of Muñoz and his followers, and because Muñoz was not pushing for independence *now,* Barceló and his faction wearily went along with the independence plank—without agreeing with it. After all, if Muñoz bolted from the party, they would have little chance of winning seats in the Puerto Rican Senate.

The subject of "status"—statehood or independence—was also being discussed by political leaders of the Socialist and the Republican parties, which was still operating as a coalition. The Republican Party was for statehood. The Socialists felt that with the people of Puerto Rico starving, illiterate, and diseased, there were plenty of election issues to deal with aside from the matter of status—which should therefore be dropped from the present political agenda.

However, there was one small party, the Nationalists, whose be-all and end-all was independence. Furthermore, they wanted independence from the United States—at once. And they insisted that the only way to get it was through armed uprising.

But in the campaign of 1932 the Nationalists used ranting words instead of bullets. And at election time they drew only 2 percent of the votes.

As had been expected, the coalition of Republican and Socialist parties won—with 54 percent of the votes. But the Liberales—the party of Muñoz and Barceló—pulled more than any other single party: 44 percent of the votes. And at age thirty-four Luis Muñoz Marín became a Senator at Large.

This title meant that he represented no particular district on the island. But he was supposed to confine his activities to the island. Muñoz, however, defined the job differently.

His first campaign did not seem of momentous importance. He went all out against slot machines and other gambling devices—which swiftly disappeared.

Then Muñoz flexed his muscles and expanded his scope—to Washington, D.C. This, of course, was supposed to be the exclusive realm of the resident commis-

Luis Muñoz Rivera, known as the "George Washington" of Puerto Rico

Doña Amalia, Muñoz's mother

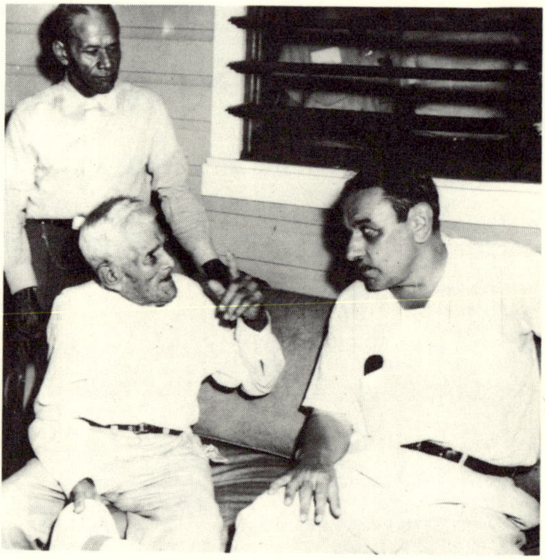

The *jíbaro* wearing a *pava* became the emblem for the Popular Democratic Party.

Muñoz would enter a town on foot, stroll through the streets, sit on a bench and talk to the people.

l. to r., Dr. Antonio Colorado, Muñoz's wife, Inés, Muñoz Marín, their daughter Viviana.

Muñoz improved conditions so that many people were able to move from wooden shacks to cement block "self-help houses."

Muñoz with children in a new low-income housing development

sioner, Santiago Iglesias. But Muñoz ran rings around the resident commissioner—in contacts, in activities, and in accomplishments.

During the Greenwich Village days Muna had become friendly with a journalist named Ruby Black. They had both been active in the women's movement. Ruby had red cheeks and brown hair drawn back from her face; she was lively and gay; and by 1932, when Senator at Large Muñoz remet her in Washington, Ruby had become friendly with the new First Lady of the land, Eleanor Roosevelt.

Muñoz made Ruby the Washington correspondent of *La Democracia*. And Ruby Black soon became known throughout the island as a true friend of Puerto Rico. She not only knew the island's problems and was sympathetic, but was in a position to help. She and Muñoz made a formidable team.

This was proved dramatically when Ruby suggested to Mrs. Roosevelt that the Puerto Rican Senator at Large be invited to tea at the White House. Mrs. Roosevelt, in turn, suggested to her husband that he might want to stop in at teatime to meet the brilliant young Muñoz. And, as Ruby, Muñoz, and the First Lady were chatting, the President of the United States was wheeled into the room.

Franklin Roosevelt had made many dramatic moves since he became President in the November, 1932, elections. He had given some hope to his countrymen that under his leadership the United States might be able to fight its way through the terrifying Depression which had spread across the entire nation. But Franklin Roosevelt had also made a few mistakes. And one of them was approving the appointment of Robert H. Gore as the American governor of Puerto Rico. There had been some good governors. There had been some bad ones like Montgomery Reilly. Of the bad ones Gore won top honors as the worst. Muñoz wanted to see Roosevelt because of Governor Gore.

The President did not have much time, for he had an, important appointment to keep with Maxim Litvinoff, the first ambassador from Communist Russia to the United States. Not knowing when the teatime would be interrupted, Muñoz launched at once into a recital of Gore's missteps and gory mistakes as governor of Puerto Rico. As one hair-raising example, Gore had demanded that all his new appointees hand in a signed and undated letter of resignation before he or she took office. In this way Gore could fire anyone at whim and at a moment's notice. This particular rule roused such a storm of resentment on the island that the governor denied ever having asked for the resignation letters. At which point Muñoz had written a fiery front-page editorial with a headline—in English—GOVERNOR GORE, YOU ARE A DAMN LIAR! Muñoz dared the governor to sue him if the resignation-letter story were *not* true.

"But," said Muñoz to President Roosevelt, "Governor Gore did not sue. Because this—and all the other things I have written about him—are true." Muñoz further pointed out that when Gore was appointed as governor he did not even know where Puerto Rico was.

Roosevelt frowned, uncomfortably. Gore had been one of the first men in the country to start the Roosevelt-for-

President boom. Furthermore, he was very wealthy and had contributed heavily to Roosevelt's campaign. The governorship of Puerto Rico had been his political payoff.

Muñoz, of course, knew this. He also knew that now he had a unique chance to speak for his people. And he must make full use of it. He knew that FDR had a good sense of humor, so he told some Governor Gore stories which might make the President laugh—and therefore listen. He told him about the governor's incompetent appointees. One of them "qualified" by having been chairman of a commission which was to propose ways to improve the island's drastic economic conditions. "He thought of a splendid idea," said Muñoz. "Buy a slew of canary birds. Teach them to sing 'The Star-Spangled Banner.' And sell them in the USA."

Roosevelt roared with laughter.

Muñoz laughed too—and then commented that *living* under the rulings of Governor Gore was no laughing matter.

By the end of teatime it was clear that Roosevelt liked and admired this charming and outspoken Luis Muñoz Marín. It was also clear that Gore would go.

The governor "resigned" soon after.

Muñoz took the steamer home and was astonished to see a cheering crowd awaiting him at the dock. With the departure of Gore the star of Luis Muñoz Marín had risen quickly. Everyone knew that it was Muñoz who had gotten rid of the hated governor. It seemed that half the city of San Juan had gathered to greet him. And the parade which followed was one of the largest and most exuberant the city had ever seen.

CHAPTER 10

Some months later Eleanor Roosevelt came to Puerto Rico. Since the U.S. President was confined to a wheelchair, he encouraged his wife to make unofficial visits abroad. She was, as he put it, "my legs."

In Puerto Rico she was escorted much of the time by Muñoz. He took her first to the most picturesque part of San Juan, the seven square blocks of the old walled city, blocks paved by brick-shaped, blue-colored stone. And he told her about the Three Musketeers who had once called this section their Blue-Brick Kingdom. He showed her the house in which he was born; 151 Fortaleza Street; and the school to which he had gone, on Calle Sol.

"How lovely," Mrs. Roosevelt said, "to go to a school on Sun Street!"

She was entranced by the old city with its narrow streets edged by thick-walled, centuries-old buildings, with their great wooden doors studded with nail designs and their wrought-iron balconies which cast lacy shadows on the sun-lined streets.

Then, abruptly, Muñoz took her to La Perla, in the northern part of Old San Juan. It lay between the Atlantic

Ocean and the old city wall. Despite its exotic name, the Pearl, it was one of the worst slums under the American flag. At the bottom of the steep hill waves slashed against rocks green with mossy slime. Many hundreds of shacks clung to the hillside; some of rotting wood, some of tin covered by old tar paper. The streets were streams of garbage and stinking sewerage; the sidewalks swaying planks resting on the refuse. Goats and pigs ambled in and out of the shanties. The screams of dying cattle from the nearby city slaughterhouse seemed the symbolic sound of the slum.

Children were everywhere, and many of them were naked.

"We don't have birth control," Muñoz remarked to Mrs. Roosevelt. "We only have death control."

He took her to other slums, still worse ones, on the mosquito-infested flats by the lagoons and the bay, shacks built on mud and hillocks of garbage. One section where the stench was unbearable had been named by the slum dwellers Buenos Aires—good air. Another was called El Fanguito, little mudhole.

Mrs. Roosevelt made sure that a number of reporters accompanied her on visits to the slums. Ruby Black later wrote:

> To the great distress of the American colony in San Juan who wanted to make Puerto Rico a rich man's playground, Mrs. Roosevelt took reporters and photographers across rickety catwalks over a dank swamp to little houses built out of debris of the 1932 hurricane, took them into the muddy alleys in sight of

> the beautiful Spanish palaces of the Governor and the Commandant of the 65th Infantry, stepped over pigs and game cocks into the six-by-nine-foot shacks in which the poor and jobless lived and died of tuberculosis and malnutrition.*

Mrs. Roosevelt, in fact, had been deeply sympathetic to the needs of Puerto Rico before she ever set foot on the island. In November, 1933, Ruby Black had written in *La Democracia,* "To her more than any other person should be attributed the increase in relief funds for the country, even though she remains in the background, shying publicity, and giving full credit to the federal administrators."

Muñoz now pointed out that the island was grateful for the relief money which had come as part of Roosevelt's New Deal. But what Puerto Rico really needed was a total plan for reconstruction. "Not aspirin but vitamins," he said.

Mrs. Roosevelt, accompanied by a few Washington experts, visited the entire island and had many meetings with Puerto Rican government leaders and economists. The result of the trip was that three of the Puerto Rican experts were invited to Washington to serve on a Puerto Rican Commission to study the matter of health, education, and job situation of the islanders. Muñoz was told that he would be "more than welcome" at all the conferences, but his participation must be "unofficial";

* Ruby Black. *Eleanor Roosevelt.* New York: Duell, Sloan and Pearce, 1940.

otherwise the official resident commissioner, Iglesias, would be embarrassed, to put it mildly.

The commission met in Washington in April and May, 1934. And Muñoz Marín was there.

On the island rumors went out, followed by faint rays of hope.

But hope could go just so far.

On June 27, 1934, Muñoz sent a telegram to the American President:

> THE PEOPLE OF PUERTO RICO ARE NOW LITERALLY LIVING ON HOPE . . . HOPE IN YOU, IN YOUR SENSE OF JUSTICE, IN YOUR RECONSTRUCTION POLICY. IF IT WEREN'T FOR THIS HOPE, NO UNEMPLOYED WORKER COULD GET A POUND OF RICE ON CREDIT AT A COUNTRY STORE, NO MORTGAGE WOULD GO UNFORECLOSED, NO CREDIT WOULD BE EXTENDED. THE ECONOMY OF THE ISLAND WOULD STOP AND BREAK DOWN.

But the President could not move too quickly. He was bound up by all sorts of legal and governmental red tape, and by pressures coming at him from all sides and all sources. If there was to be a Reconstruction Plan for Puerto Rico, various opposing forces wanted a piece of the action and a piece of the pie. Roosevelt was, however, able to push through a few proposals. One of these was that Puerto Rico would no longer be under the U.S. War Department—where it had been ever since the Spanish-American War. It was now moved over to the Department of the Interior, headed by Harold Ickes, who was sympathetic to the needs of the island.

Muñoz found that he could find his way around with far greater ease in the offices of the Interior Department than in the cold-shouldering military offices of the War Department. And soon, working day and night, Muñoz became the greatest lobbyist the Puerto Rican people ever had in Washington, talking with politicians to further the cause of Puerto Rican reconstruction.

But still, by Christmastime no Reconstruction Plan for the island had emerged.

On December 13, 1934, Muñoz sent the President a letter which said, in part, "Puerto Ricans are now going through more hell than it has even been their fate to experience before . . . one million two hundred thousand in need of relief. . . . My appeal to you, Mr. President, is for reassurance to my people . . . so that they can tighten their belts and wait for justice."

The President's answer to this letter was revealed to the Puerto Rican public in a dramatic and surprising way.

On the evening of December 22, 1934, a radio was placed in every plaza in every town and city in Puerto Rico. Radios were also set up on crossroads throughout the country. Loudspeakers were attached to each radio. It was estimated that a half million people (about a fourth of the island population) gathered to hear the message. What they heard was the voice of Luis Muñoz Marín, from Washington, translating the President's letter to him: "I can and do assure you and your people of my complete goodwill and firm determination that permanent reconstruction shall be initiated at the very earliest possible moment."

Two days later Muñoz wrote to the President that, in Puerto Rico, as a result of the broadcast, "public feeling has turned from despair to exultant Christmas cheer."*

Almost one year to the day after the removal of General Gore, Muñoz returned to Puerto Rico, more of a hero than ever.

A new federal agency had been created in the United States: the Puerto Rico Reconstruction Administration. It had an operating fund of $40,000,000. The PRRA would be headed by an American, Dr. Ernest Gruening (who became interested in Puerto Rico when he was editor of *The Nation* and had bought many articles about the island from the young writer Luis Muñoz Marín).

The PRRA was opposed viciously and violently by the sugar barons and by the coalition politicians who, shortsightedly, saw it as a huge waving feather in the cap of the leading Liberal Party man, Luis Muñoz Marín. But to the people of Puerto Rico, the PRRA seemed like a miracle. For centuries they had been accustomed to being both ignored and exploited—first by Spain, then by the United States. Now, for the first time, they would be helped directly by the United States. And they would be helped to help themselves.

Although Muñoz refused any official position in the PRRA, he did more than any other person to bring the plan to the people, explain it to them, and win their

* Franklin D. Roosevelt Library, letter from Luis Muñoz Marín to President Roosevelt, December 24, 1934.

backing. Again, he spent days and nights speaking in all parts of the island.

He told them that the PRRA would break up the great sugar estates and return the land to the people. He told them about the PRRA's plan to bring electricity to all the homes on the island. He explained how the PRRA would foster industry in the cities and create new jobs. "The extent to which you now support the PRRA," he said, "is also the extent to which you support a brighter future for yourselves and your children."

Throughout the island the PRRA came to be thought of as the creation of Luis Muñoz Marín. He was loved and respected for himself and for what he was doing for the people; not because he was the son of Luis Muñoz Rivera.

As a sign of his importance it was rumored that the sugar barons were planning to have him killed. Friends of Muñoz took to carrying revolvers to protect him. Even he carried a gun in his pocket when he sat in cafés, or town plazas, or when he made speeches discussing and defending the plans and policies of the PRRA.

As it turned out, it was a bullet which sent Muñoz from the summit to the depths in a matter of months. But the bullet was not aimed at him.

CHAPTER 11

The leader of the Puerto Rican Nationalist Party was a brilliant, dynamic, and dangerous man named Pedro Albizu Campos. Despite the fact that his party had won only 2 percent of the votes in the 1932 election, and thereafter never received enough names on a petition to appear again on the ballot, Albizu acted as if he were the president of Puerto Rico.

He dressed impressively in a dark suit, white shirt, black Homburg hat, and black tie. And he was an impressive speaker. His deep baritone voice carried far without a microphone; his diction was perfect. He could enthrall an audience. Sometimes, when Albizu spoke of the American dominators of Puerto Rico, his voice rose to a shrill scream of hatred.

Most of his followers were young men of fifteen to twenty-five. They wore uniforms consisting of black shirt, white tie, and white trousers. They called themselves the Army of Liberation.

One Sunday morning, February 23, 1936, the American chief of police on the island, Colonel E. Francis Riggs, was on his way home from mass, which he always attended at the ancient Cathedral of San Juan Bautista, in the old walled city. His habits were well known. At noon every Sunday he left the cathedral, got into his chauffeur-driven car, and drove through the narrow, nearly deserted streets of the city to the Escabron Beach Club, where he lived.

On this particular sunny Sunday morning, a young man in a white linen suit stood in a doorway on Allen Street. When the colonel's car passed, the young man stepped onto the running board and shot Riggs in the chest. He then raced away, followed on foot by Riggs' chauffeur, who was armed. He was caught and taken to police headquarters.

Riggs, meanwhile, was trying to stop the flow of blood from his chest when another young man stepped up to the car and called out to Riggs, "Colonel, I saw everything. I'll act as a witness."

Riggs turned to answer, whereupon the second young man shot the colonel twice in the head. Riggs died at once.

This assailant also was caught and taken to the police station. There both young men stated that they were Nationalists. They seemed surprised at their arrest. They were not, after all, killing Puerto Ricans. "We must all join to kill the Americans," one of them explained to the police.

What happened inside the police station after that was never revealed. But the two young men were killed there.

The island was stunned by the murder of Riggs. They also took note of the death of the murderers in the police station. The Nationalists declared the assassins were martyrs. They swore to avenge the deaths of the two young men. And Albizu declared that every man who wore the uniform of the Insular Police was a murderer.

Tension and fear spread throughout the cities and villages.

And shock and horror spread through Washington. People failed to realize that the Nationalists represented only a tiny fragment of the Puerto Rican population. All Puerto Ricans were lumped together in angry blame.

Dr. Gruening, head of the PRRA, suggested to his old friend Muñoz that the Senator at Large issue a statement condemning the assassination of Riggs. It was necessary, said Gruening, to make it clear at once that the Puerto Rican people, as such, were in no way behind the murder of Riggs. And Muñoz, as the political figure most known in Washington, was the obvious man to make such a statement.

Muñoz replied that the murder was a terrible thing which could have serious consequences for all Puerto Ricans. But the killing of the two assassins without a trial was also terrible, and he could not publicly condemn the one without also condemning the other. He told Gruening. "I will gladly make a strong statement about Riggs' assassination if you will make a parallel statement about the lynching of the assassins."

Gruening refused. And from that moment on, Muñoz found that Gruening's friendship for him had cooled. And that, as a result, Washington doors which had been wide open to him were starting to close.

At that time Ruby Black was in the hospital in Washington. Muñoz and Gruening came to see her at different times. Gruening paced the floor and announced, "But, Ruby, he is condoning murder!" And during *his* visits Muñoz pointed out, "If I did what Gruening asked I would be committing political suicide."

Ruby later wrote that if she had been feeling fit she might have prevented this important political and social friendship from breaking up. But she did not prevent it.

And by the time Muñoz sailed for Puerto Rico he was no longer "in" in Washington. He was very clearly "out."

Furthermore, he returned to an island seething in chaos, confusion, and anger.

Senator Millard Tydings of Maryland had been a close friend of Colonel Riggs. Indeed, it was Tydings who had suggested Riggs for the position of police chief of Puerto Rico. Tydings was chairman of the Senate committee which handled Puerto Rican affairs in Congress. And he promptly introduced a bill granting Puerto Rico immediate independence.

Although a vast number of Puerto Ricans, like Muñoz, favored eventual independence for the island, they certainly did not want it at once, and on the terms put forth in the Tydings Bill, which gave the island almost no time to adjust its economy. All the ties which attached it to the United States would be cut almost at once. They thought immediate independence would mean disaster and starvation for the island.

Muñoz summed up the bill by saying that it was a return to the old Mexican *ley de fuga*, or law of flight, under which the police used to arrest someone, tell him kindly to take off, and shoot him in the back for trying to escape.

It was hard for people at home to believe that Muñoz, who had always been at the center of the Washington world, knew nothing about the Tydings Bill until it was brought up in Congress. This was, in fact, the case. But Muñoz understood the futility of trying to make the islanders realize that he was now an outsider on the Washington scene. When he returned home he found that he had lost power, prestige, and following. And he discovered that his own Liberal party was split about how to react politically to the Tydings Bill. Some said they must take independence while it was offered, despite the drastic outcomes. Some said independence was worthless if it came hand in hand with economic disaster.

Muñoz felt that since the party was split and uncertain, they should stay out of the November elections. After the elections they should work for independence *with* all the proper guarantees for economic protection. Barceló announced that this plan of staying away from the polls would mean political suicide for the party. And Muñoz finally said that he would abide by the vote of the party leaders as to whether or not the Liberal Party should appear on the ticket, but that he would not run for office.

The Liberal Party convention was held in July, 1936. After fiery debates a vote was taken at three o'clock in the morning. The vote for the Muñoz Plan—the withdrawal of the Liberal Party from the November elections—was 101. The vote favoring the Liberal Party's entry in the elections was 101. According to rules, the party chairman was asked to cast the deciding vote. The chairman was Barceló. He voted against Luis Muñoz Marín.

Muñoz wrote to Ruby Black, "I believe that the convention defeated Puerto Rico by one vote. It certainly did not defeat me."

But he was wrong.

Although the Liberal Party got 48 percent of the votes in the 1936 elections, the coalition of Socialists and Republicans still held power. Barceló announced that had it not been for the Muñoz Plan, which split the Liberal Party down the middle, they would have won the election. Therefore, the Central Executive Committee had decreed that Luis Muñoz Marín could no longer speak for the Liberal Party.

Muñoz and his closest followers were expelled from the party. Muñoz then returned to Washington to fight for Puerto Rican independence—with economic safeguards.

The Tydings Bill was defeated in Congress, but Luis Muñoz Marín had nothing to do with that victory.

In Washington he found all important doors closed to him. He was a man without a party. He had no influence. He was Mr. Nobody.

Furthermore, the Muñoz marriage was heading for disaster. He and Muna had separated. She had taken the two children to live with her near the University of Puerto Rico, where she worked.

Within eight months Luis Muñoz Marín had plummeted from the summits as the most important and respected Puerto Rican on the island and on the Mainland to the depths. He was, at the age of thirty-eight, a man defeated on all fronts, a man who faced despair.

CHAPTER 12

It seemed impossible that a man could fall so far, so fast.

Muñoz supporters in the PRRA suddenly began receiving pink slips: notifications that they were fired. A stench of fear arose. Even those men and women who wanted to continue their friendship with him did not dare to, not if their jobs might be threatened by it. Some of his braver "supporters" would park their cars blocks away from his house and sneak in the back way.

Finally, in 1938, after months of inner turmoil and indecision, Muñoz made a surprising announcement: he would start a new political party. A party of the people, El Partido Popular Democrático—the Popular Democratic Party.

But starting a new party was far easier said than done.

In order to get on the ballot in the forthcoming 1940 elections, thousands of petitions favoring the new party had to be signed in each of the 786 voting districts in the land—and each signature had to be witnessed by a judge!

The very idea of a new party rang out with the word *impossible*.

Over half the people in Puerto Rico were illiterate. They could not put their signature on a petition even if they wanted to. And for those who could sign a paper, how to manage the judge-witness? There were only a handful of judges in each voting district, and they were busy, affluent men. None was about to tour around the countryside with a penniless Muñoz in order to witness signatures on a piece of paper—should anyone be persuaded to sign it.

Muñoz thought of a poem his father had once written: "Sisyphus." In this Puerto Rican version of the Greek legend, Sisyphus, with great effort, finally managed to shove a gigantic boulder all the way to the top of a huge mountain. And while he stood in the warming sunlight, bathing in the cheers and adulation of the people far below, the mountain suddenly shook in an earthquake. And the boulder crashed down the mountainside till it lay where Sisyphus first found it.

> In this, the bitter struggle of our sterile strife,
> Behold, entire, the story of the poet's life.

Or, reflected Muñoz Marín, the politician's life.

But he was not quite alone in the bitter struggle. There were a few friends in San Juan who backed him. And there were the *jíbaros* of the hills. Most of them had never heard of PRRA, of Dr. Gruening, or of power politics on the island and on the Mainland. But they all knew the name of Luis Muñoz Rivera. And they remembered Luis Muñoz Marín from the campaigns of 1932 and 1936. They remembered him and they trusted him.

Muñoz decided to start his campaign at the top of the mountain—in his father's hometown, Barranquitas.

But a party needed more than a philosophy and a name.

It needed a sign, a symbol, which people who could not read would easily comprehend.

One of the friends who had stuck by Muñoz was a handsome young political writer named Antonio Colorado.

On a hot spring afternoon Colorado was in the office of *La Democracia* working on a free-lance article for the paper when Muñoz called him over. "Antonio, I have an idea for an emblem for the party. But I can't draw. Make a few sketches, will you? The face of a *jíbaro*. And underneath it the words *Pan-Tierra-Libertad.*" (Bread-Land-Liberty)

Colorado returned to his table, did a few drawings, and in a matter of minutes brought them back to Muñoz.

"This one," said Muñoz Marín, selecting the profiled face of a *jíbaro* wearing a large straw hat, round-crowned, broad-brimmed, a *pava,* the typical hat of the Puerto Rican men of the hills.

"Now go across the street," Muñoz said, "to the photoengraving shop. Ask Paco to do the engraving for me."

Thus, the party acquired its symbol and slogan.

But it needed more than that to win a place on the ballot.

Night after night Muñoz and a handful of loyal friends sat in his office in *La Democracia* to work out a platform. Most of the "regulars" were men. But there were several women.

Puerto Rican women had been given the vote for the first time in the 1932 elections. And now there were women who did far more than vote. There was Felisa Rincón, who worked in her own dress shop all day and came to political meetings at night. And there was Inés María Mendoza de Palacios: warm, vibrant, fiery, and beautiful.

She was the wife of Rafael Palacios, a brilliant artist who worked on the *Puerto Rico Herald,* an English-language newspaper in San Juan.

Muñoz had known about Inés before he met her. Indeed, he had written many stories about her in *La Democracia*. Inés had been a high school teacher, and like virtually all teachers in Puerto Rico, she condemned the American-imposed ruling that all students must be taught in English. The island culture was Spanish, Inés insisted, and should remain so. She had the courage to speak up on this matter before an official commission. Her comments received much newspaper coverage, and she received more coverage still when her contract was not renewed and she was thrown out of the public-school teaching system.

Muñoz agreed with her stand about preserving the Spanish culture in Puerto Rico. And when he met her he found that he agreed with her about many things. He also found that he was falling in love. But he tried his best to shove this matter from his mind. If he planned to found a new political party and start a new political life, about the last thing he needed was to fall in love with a married woman.

At the late-night sessions Muñoz and his followers hammered out twenty-two points which would become their platform, should they become a party. Then the twenty-two points were printed. Muñoz planned to hand them out to people as a scorecard. "Check our actions against our promises," he would tell the voters. "When we are elected—keep score."

When we are elected . . .

Other politicians who heard of the new party scoffed. They well knew the impossibility of getting 53,000 petitions signed and witnessed by judges in 786 election districts. But if Muñoz wanted to try this madness, it was all very well with them. Each felt that if Muñoz succeeded in getting on the ballot in some districts he would merely draw votes from *their* opponents. Most politicians agreed with the summation of the noted Puerto Rican historian Arturo Morales Carrion, who wrote, "Muñoz, who for a moment had been the great promise, disappears from the urban scene. His star is in deep eclipse, and he is now seen only as the leader of a routed faction, a political Bohemian who had pilfered the treasure of a name and an illustrious tradition."

There was, therefore, some surprise when on July 22, 1938, Muñoz announced that his new Popular Party had enough judge-witnessed signatures to appear on the ballot in Barranquitas and Luquillo.

Well, everyone said, Barranquitas—naturally the son of Muñoz Rivera would be bound to get signatures there!

But Luquillo—how had he done it in Luquillo?

He did it by means which had never before been used on the island.

He had an old Ford with the license plate 447. He would chug up a mountain, park the car, and wander into a village. He would remain there for several days, sleeping in a hammock in a *jíbaro's* shack, wandering around, talking to the people—not talking at them or above them—talking with them, finding out how they felt and letting them know that how they felt he felt.

He learned soon enough that the people in the hills were not the slightest bit interested in the matter which was tearing political parties apart, status—whether Puerto Rico would have independence or statehood. They were interested in their annual income. (The "dead season" in the sugarcane fields—the starvation season—lasted a long seven months.) They were interested in getting food for their stomachs, clothes for their backs, and new roofs for their shacks. And they were very interested in the $2 which came so easily every four years when every man, and now every woman, too, could sell a vote.

Muñoz decided that *his* party would drop status as an issue. *Jalda Arriba!* became the slogan. *Up the hill!*

How to get there?

"Don't sell your vote!" cried Muñoz, over and over, to people who stared at him and made no reply. Naturally they thought, the Popular Party said, "Don't sell your vote." The reason was simple: the Popular Party had no money to *buy* votes!

But this was not the reason. And Muñoz and the party members who echoed his words in other villages had to find a way to make people believe this.

Finally Muñoz found the way. "*Lend* me your vote—just once!" he would cry. "Then I will be in debt—to *you!*

Once I am in office, watch what I do for you. See if your wages go up. See if there is more food on your stove. See if I keep my promises to you. If I don't—all right, in the next election you are free to sell your vote again. But this time give my party a chance to help you. That's all we ask for, a chance to help!"

This seemed a fair proposal to fair-minded men. And many nodded now when Muñoz spoke. They were with him.

The boulder which Sisyphus shoved became easier to push up the hill. More and more workers, young, idealistic, joined the Popular Party.

Muñoz had no money to pay any of them. He could not even pay their expenses. Or his own. At one (typical) point, after a speech he said to his driver, "How much money do you have?"

"Seventeen cents."

"Good," said Party Leader Muñoz. "I have nine cents. Get all the gasoline the money will buy and drive as far as it will take us. Maybe somebody will help us out on the other end."

Said the driver, "When do we eat? And on what?"

Muñoz shrugged. "Maybe somebody will feed us."

And usually somebody did.

He managed to turn the fact that his party was poverty-stricken into a political advantage. He would take up collections among the *jíbaros*—a few pennies here, five cents there—enough to buy gas to get him on to the next town. But he took care to point out that the Popular Party was the people's own party, supported by them. The other parties were supported by the sugar barons and other wealthy men. Those party leaders had to "pay back" their benefactors when they got into power.

"That," said Muñoz, "is why you have seen many political parties win—while *you* have never won."

He spoke to small groups in homes, in fields, in village plazas. Once, in the mountains, he was scheduled to speak and only one *jíbaro* was there to hear him. "Gather some more people," said Muñoz.

The man said, "Speak to *me*."

Said Muñoz, "But—you're only one."

The *jíbaro* answered, "Don't forget, with one you start counting."

So Muñoz spoke to the one *jíbaro* about the minimum wage law and land reform. He taught the man to write his name so that he could sign the petition asking that the Popular Party be put on the ballot. And he drove the *jíbaro* to a nearby town so his signature could be witnessed by a judge.

It was true: with one you start counting. But the party needed 50,000 more votes before they could appear on the ballots throughout the island. And there were so few party workers and so little time.

Was he shoving the boulder up the hill night and day, only to have it crash down to the bottom again before election day?

CHAPTER 13

Impossibilities were overcome in impossible ways.

There was no money to print leaflets explaining the stand of the *Populares*. In any case, the majority of the *jíbaros* could not read. Nor did the hill people own radios. So Muñoz and his followers, trying to reach as many as they could in the months which grew ever shorter, stood on hilltops and shouted their speeches through megaphones.

Other political parties distributed campaign buttons and emblems. The *Populares* had no money for this. So they went about the land with pots of paint and brushes and adorned huge boulders and old walls with the profile of the *jíbaro* wearing a *pava*.

Muñoz kept going day and night, speaking in every election district on the island, and then returning to speak again. He never hurried through a speech. And at most of the *Populares'* meetings the listeners also spoke—and the speakers learned.

Muñoz later wrote, "I learned there is a wisdom among the people in the towns and countryside which education may lead, but cannot improve. I taught many of them something, but they taught me more.

"I learned that the people are wise—wiser than we think. I learned that to them freedom is something deep in the heart, in the conscience, in everyday life. I also learned that the great majority of the people of Puerto Rico prefer close association with their fellow citizens of the American Union, and with all men on earth, to the bitter narrowness of separation."

During his grueling trek through the hills and mountains of Puerto Rico, Muñoz dropped the idea of independence for Puerto Rico from his political campaigning. He had learned this lesson from the *jíbaros*.

Slowly the boulder being shoved up the mountain grew lighter as more and more joined the *Populares*. Certain judges became interested in Muñoz: his new methods of campaigning; the honesty he preached; and the hope he promised. They agreed to stay late in their offices and a car pool system was organized. Muñoz's rattling old Ford, and any other car or truck which could be mustered, entered towns and cities at night crammed full with men and women of the mountains, who had come to have their signatures witnessed on the *Populares'* petition. Then, singing and shouting, they were driven home again.

But, Muñoz often wondered, had they come for a free trip to town or because they understood and believed in what he and his party members were saying?

Then came some real hope that the *jíbaros* wanted to hear what Muñoz was saying—and would take risks to do so. A sugar baron who lived in Jajome became worried about the message that Muñoz was preaching. This madman Muñoz wanted to enforce the dusty old 500-Acre Law which had been carefully forgotten by island politicians for decades. Under this law no corporation was permitted to own or control more than 500 acres of Puerto Rican land. But by 1939 over half the suitable farmland on the island was controlled by a half dozen corporations. Now Muñoz was preaching that the law should be enforced and the land returned to the *jibaros*! Naturally the sugar barons regarded this idea as dangerous inflammatory insanity. They understood that Muñoz could never be elected. But they did not want workers to become upset by listening to such ideas. So the Jajome landowner called his overseer to his splendid mountain villa and gave orders: "No one is to go to the Muñoz rally tonight!"

The overseer passed the message on to the cane cutters. Since they all lived on the vast plantation, he could do more than give out orders. He locked the gate so they *could* not disobey. But that night the *jíbaros* cut a hole in the fence, and at the risk of their jobs 200 of them showed up at the rally.

Muñoz, too, took some risks. A rally was scheduled one night in the village of Playa Cortada. Muñoz's car was stopped on the road by a guard with a gun. The sugar *central* owned all the land around Playa Cortada. The sugar baron had given orders that Muñoz could not trespass.

But there was a stream nearby. Streams and rivers were not private property. They were in the public domain. So Muñoz took off his shoes, rolled up his well-worn khaki trousers, and waded his way into Playa Cortada, where a crowd was waiting to hear him.

In one election district after another the *Populares* collected enough judge-witnessed signatures to appear on the ballot. Then Muñoz and his party workers, who now numbered some 4,000, moved down to the cities. Instead of mountaintop meetings with crowds of several hundred, they could address thousands of people at once.

Then, on September 15, in Santurce, the suburb of San Juan in which his father had died, Luis Muñoz Marín organized another "political first." A mass meeting was held, attended by 15,000 people. Every Popular candidate for the Puerto Rican House or Senate came up to the stage and one by one, took a solemn oath to vote for each of the twenty-two bills which the party would put through if it were elected. Political promises were old hat in political campaigns, but this, an oath, was something new. And word of the Santurce oath taking spread throughout the island.

Muñoz believed in the people. Did the people believe Muñoz?

By election night the Popular Party had won its place on the ballot in each of the 786 voting districts in the country. In many districts they had achieved twice as many signatures as they needed to appear on the ballot.

Signatures were one thing. Votes were another.

Would the people continue to sell their votes? Some *jíbaros* had hinted that they would accept the $2 bribe, but would vote for Muñoz. He had discouraged this. "You can't have two dollars—and justice," he told them.

Complete election honesty was the cornerstone for building an honest government, a government truly for the people.

On election eve, November 5, 1940, Muñoz sat in his second-floor office listening to the early election returns. Only one friend was with him, Jorge Font Saldaña, who had quit his PRRA job in 1936 in protest of Dr. Gruening's treatment of Muñoz. Since then Jorge had been unable to find steady work; at times his family went hungry.

Both men were exhausted. Muñoz had spent 837 days and nights touring the island. Almost two solid years and four months. He claimed to have seen more Puerto Ricans than anyone alive. And no one disputed this.

Where was the boulder? Tonight would it crash to the bottom of the mountain again?

Early returns started coming in.

Bayamón, a Republican stronghold. Naturally the *Populares* could not make a showing in Bayamón.

Then Muñoz stood up and turned the radio louder. The *Populares* were winning in Bayamón!

Returns came in from Coamo, another Republican stronghold. The *Populares* were winning there, too!

The polls throughout the country had closed at two P.M. By six that evening a good cross section of the returns were in. The hill districts were voting solidly Popular.

Luis Muñoz Marín looked at his friend Jorge. There were tears on Jorge's cheeks.

"They are not selling their votes," Muñoz said quietly. "Jorge, the *jíbaros* are not selling their votes!"

Other party workers burst into the office, shouting with excitement.

They listened all night.

By dawn the next morning almost all the results were in.

The *Populares* had won 38 percent of the votes. In the House of Representatives they had won eighteen seats. The coalition had also won eighteen seats. The *Populares* had won ten of the nineteen Senate seats. There they had a majority of one.

Bolívar Pagán, a Socialist, had been elected resident commissioner.

But the new president of the Puerto Rican Senate, the most important man on the island, was Luis Muñoz Marín.

CHAPTER 14

Don Luis, as people now called him, had lost one battle; with himself. In fact, he had made very little effort to win it.

The beautiful, fiery Inés Mendoza became his common-law wife. Several days after the victorious election campaign of 1940 she gave birth to a baby girl, their second daughter. The first, born in 1939, was called Viviana. The name of the second baby was an obvious one: Victoria.

Muñoz, Inés, and the two tiny girls moved to Isla Verde, near San Juan, where they lived in a wooden house hidden in a palm grove.

Muna and the two older children lived near the university, many miles away. Muñoz and Muna. Once they had been one; their names had been said as one. Now they were officially separated.

In 1947 Muna and Muñoz were divorced. And Inés Mendoza became Señora Inés Mendoza de Muñoz Marín.

During those years Muñoz had become the most important man in Puerto Rican history.

His father had won self-rule from Spain and had been responsible for the historic Jones Bill. But Luis Muñoz Marín, as head of the Puerto Rican Senate, had managed to push through twenty-two historic bills, which dramatically bettered the life of over 80 percent of the islanders: the city poor and the country poor.

This not only was done speedily, but was done at the constant risk to the life of a tall, thin, mild-mannered man named Dr. Rafael Arrillaga Torrens.

Before the 1940 election Muñoz had handed out thousands of "scorecards" so that voters could keep track of whether or not his party got all twenty-two bills passed. But after the 1940 election the *Populares* faced one momentous problem—the tie vote in the House of Representatives. Eighteen *Populares*. Eighteen from the coalition. Each party voted as a bloc. And nothing could be passed unless someone from the coalition changed his vote and joined the *Populares*. Night after night Muñoz bought time on the radio and pleaded with the people of Puerto Rico to send letters and telegrams to their coalition representatives insisting that they vote for the twenty-two bills of the *Populares*. "*Falta un hombre*!" became his plea, his slogan. We need one man!

Dr. Arrillaga turned out to be that man. He was a coalition representative, but he began to vote for the *Populares'* bills. And some were swiftly passed. Free lunches for schoolchildren. New housing for slum dwellers. Electricity and running water for 150 rural districts. New medical centers.

But there was a ruling in the legislature. If one of their

House or Senate members died, the party could promptly appoint a successor. If Dr. Arrillaga died—or was killed—this wild flood of *Populares'* bills could be stopped.

A man was given $1,000 and a revolver to do the job. But he muffed it. Would this threat to his life make the doctor stop voting with the *Populares*?

Two policemen were assigned to Dr. Arrillaga day and night. He kept on voting for the *Populares'* bills. There were more attempts to murder him. One morning the doctor, driving from his office through the narrow streets of old San Juan, was shot at by two gunmen. They missed. And that day the minimum wage bill was passed.

There were twelve more attempts on his life. Each day that he survived, one or more bills were passed.

At last the killers were called off. There would be no point now in murdering Dr. Arrillaga, since other members of the coalition had started to switch to the Muñoz bandwagon.

Finally the scorecard was complete. All twenty-two bills that the *Populares* had promised the people were passed.

But passing bills was only the first step. How to implement this wave of reforms? How to pay for them?

Money came suddenly from an unexpected source.

On December 7, 1941, the United States entered World War II. Almost overnight Puerto Rico became a huge Army, Navy and Air Force base. Thousands of new jobs were created. But the most important source of new island funds came from rum, a by-product of Puerto

Rico's major industry: sugar. Because of the war, imported scotch was not available in the United States. So rum became the new U.S. drink. A popular song was heard on jukeboxes throughout the land: "Rum and Coca-Cola." The U.S. Congress generously decreed that all taxes collected on Puerto Rican rum should be returned to Puerto Rico. As one noted journalist put it, "Rum became the *spirit* behind the island's Quiet Revolution."

But the Quiet Revolution, as it was called in Washington and on the island, required more than money to get the twenty-two bills off the ground and into action. Know-how was needed. And Washington helped there, too. In 1941 Roosevelt appointed an intellectual and idealist professor, Rexford Guy Tugwell, as the new governor of Puerto Rico.

Tugwell had toured Puerto Rico with Mrs. Roosevelt in 1934. Since then he had been a real friend of the island and knew its problems well. Furthermore, he was a brilliant economist with experience in getting plans off the drawing board and into action.

Tugwell and Muñoz admired each other and worked well together. And they *did* work—twelve, fourteen, sometimes eighteen hours a day. They were a strange-looking team. Muñoz was tall and heavyset, with a stubby black mustache. He had large, brooding, dark eyes, which seemed sad even when he laughed, and a generally messy look. As president of the Senate, he wore the same type of clothes he had worn when speaking to the *jíbaros* in the hills: creased khaki pants and rumpled white shirt without a tie. Tugwell, on the other hand, was tall, slender, movie-star handsome, and always impeccably dressed.

Together, in the space of five years, the two men helped create a new countrywide health service, new roads, new homes for the poor, new power plants, new schools, and new jobs. They set up a Transportation Authority, a Housing Authority, and reorganized the Water Resources Authority. But their most far-reaching accomplishment was land reform. A new government Land Authority bought land from the huge sugar corporations, most of which were owned by Americans. *Jíbaros* who continued to work on these government-owned sugar *centrals* were given their own small plots of land to farm for themselves. In the widespread *Parceles* program, thousands of small parcels of land were either leased out to the formerly landless peasant for his lifetime or were sold for one dollar. These quarter-acre plots were enough to hold a small house and a large vegetable garden. The land was moving back into the hands of "the man with the hoe."

In the 1944 national election the Popular Party won by much more than a landslide. It was called "a Popular hurricane." All but two members of the House and two of the Senate were *Populares*. Barceló had died, and the Socialist Party had disappeared. The only other party to survive—gasping for life—was the Republican Party.

The following year, for the first time in the island's history, President Truman appointed a Puerto Rican governor for the island. His name was Jesús Piñero. He was one of Muñoz's earliest and most ardent followers.

Muñoz, Piñero, and others decided that the island could

not live on agriculture alone. There must be industry. Mainland businessmen still thought of Puerto Rico as the "Poorhouse of the Caribbean." They were not about to sink their money into the "cesspool." So the Puerto Rican government built its own factories, Rum needed bottles, so they put up a glass factory and next to it a box factory. They built a shoe factory, a cement factory, and a clay-products factory to manufacture sinks and toilet bowls for the government's new low-cost housing developments.

The five factories, however, were not notably successful, and they employed only a few hundred people. Government money, it was felt, could be better spent elsewhere. So, the government sold its five factories to a Puerto Rican businessman—and Republican—Luis Ferré.

With the money from the factory sale the government started *Fomento* (more formally known as the Economic Development Administration) a new agency to "foment" industry on the island, chiefly by encouraging a large influx of outside capital.

They offered inducements to Mainland businessmen: ten years without taxation, cheaper labor than in the United States and, that not-to-be-sniffed-at, built-in asset, the climate. Mainland businessmen began to respond, and small factories started sprouting up throughout the island.

Then the head of *Fomento,* Teodoro Moscoso, put up a five-million-dollar hotel, with 300 rooms, lush tropical gardens, and pools replete with swans and pink flamingos.

The country was horrified. What a waste of government money! The huge hotel was dubbed "Moscoso's Folly." But Conrad Hilton took it over and named it the Caribe Hilton. The hotel made a million dollars the first year and kept on earning. Furthermore, it put Puerto Rico in the tourist business. Other lush hotels were built along the beautiful beachfronts, and tourism was soon earning the island $140 million a year.

"Operation Bootstrap" Muñoz called the new industrial effort.

Not only was the island pulling itself up by its own bootstraps, but virtually every Puerto Rican was learning something as he or she pulled.

"Give a man a fish," Muñoz said, "and he will have one meal. But teach him *how* to fish, and he can eat for the rest of his life."

Puerto Ricans were taught how to help themselves and one another and did so—for the most part—without pay. The government would put up the foundations and roof of a new school. In the evenings the parents gathered and were taught how to put up the walls. A village which had only outhouses was supplied with a free septic tank for each home. And every family was taught how to dig the hole for its tank and pour the cement.

Then Muñoz started another "operation" of quite a different sort: a cultural revolution. Operation Serenity it was called.

"We don't want U.S.-style cafeterias," said Muñoz. "We want to keep our Old World-type cafés." He was horrified by the new language "Spanglish" displayed proudly on signs throughout towns and villages. HAGA SU LAUNDRY AQUÍ . . . SPECIAL SHOW ESTA NOCHE.

Operation Serenity aimed at restoring and spreading all that was best in the old Spanish and Puerto Rican culture—fighting off the "jukebox culture" which had started to pervade the island. Spanish, not English, was the language in schools. Old folk dances were revived; traveling troupes of actors went out to perform works by Spanish and Puerto Rican playwrights. Museums were built to display the work of noted Spanish and Puerto Rican artists. Ancient Spanish-built buildings and convents were carefully restored. And, later, the Institute of Puerto Rican Culture was founded to see that Spanish culture continued to flourish on the island.

Then, in 1947, there came an announcement from Washington which led to the biggest day in the life of Luis Muñoz Marín.

CHAPTER 15

The news from Washington made Muñoz remember vividly that afternoon thirty-one years and several lifetimes ago when he—seventeen-year-old-Luisito—sat in the visitors' gallery as his father, the resident commissioner, asked the U.S. Congress to amend the Jones Bill so that every Puerto Rican man on the island could vote for his representatives in the Puerto Rican House and Senate.

Now the President of the United States had announced that the Jones Bill was being amended once more. Every man and woman of voting age in Puerto Rico would be able to vote for the island's next governor in the November, 1948, elections.

There was no doubt in anyone's mind as to who the next governor would be.

On Inauguration Day, January 2, 1949, the city of San Juan seemed to be splitting at the seams. Over 200,000 people were there to see the inaugural parade and ceremonies. It turned into a week-long fiesta, complete with balls, beach picnics, horse races, and cockfights. Gaity reigned in every side street.

The mayor of San Juan had seen to it that the city was decorated with flowers, flags, bunting, and floodlights which lit up historic buildings and plazas in the nighttime. The mayor was Felisa Rincón de Gautier, one of the first women to become a dedicated Muñoz follower when he founded the *Populares* in 1938. Only ten years previously. Had any country ever been transformed so far and so fast in the space of a single decade?

The new governor—the first to be elected by the people of Puerto Rico—took the history-making oath of office, and he spoke the words slowly, forcefully, solemnly.

But Luis Muñoz Marín started his inaugural address by saying that taking an oath was not necessary.

"With oath or without it," he declared—and his words rang out across the island on radios in homes and cafés, on loudspeakers set up in plazas in every city, town, and village—"with oath or without it, forces of my inner self have wished me to make of my life an oath of service to my people."

Foreign correspondents who covered the inauguration called Muñoz the miracle man who had remade Puerto Rico.

But Muñoz saw not only what had been done—his eyes were on the yawning chasm ahead. When one reporter doing a glowing story on Operation Bootstrap asked the new governor, "Where do you go from here, sir?" Muñoz answered, "Wait a minute. We're not 'here' yet!"

A year later there came another echo from the past. But this time the echo exploded into terror.

Millard Tydings had introduced a second bill in which Puerto Rico was to vote as to whether or not it wanted independence from the United States. The lesson Muñoz had learned from the *jíbaros* of the hills in his 1940 campaign had been reinforced daily. He was convinced that the island was not economically ready for independence and that, furthermore, the majority of the islanders were proud of being Americans. He therefore followed in his father's footsteps once more. When the second Tydings Bill was defeated, Muñoz put forth the idea first presented to Congress by his father. The status of the island should be based on the Lord Durham Report, which had resulted in the Dominion of Canada. He remembered the hundreds of letters his father had written to U.S. Congressmen suggesting that Puerto Rico be moved up from the status of colony to that of Dominion or Commonwealth.

Luis Muñoz Marín began writing letters as well as visiting countless U.S. Congressmen.

On July 3, 1950, the U.S. Congress passed Public Law 600, which recommended that Puerto Rico be accorded Commonwealth status—with its own constitution approved by its own legislature. Puerto Ricans would not vote in Mainland elections. On the other hand, they would continue to be free from federal income taxes. Aside from the taxes, the U.S. government agencies would operate in Puerto Rico as in any of the separate states of the Union. The Commonwealth of Puerto Rico would be "a new kind of state."

But the Commonwealth would not come into being unless the people of Puerto Rico wanted it. And this would be decided by an islandwide vote on the matter to be held on June 4, 1951.

Since Muñoz spoke out so strongly for the Commonwealth idea, and since the people felt so strongly pro-Muñoz, there was little doubt that the idea would be approved by the people of Puerto Rico.

There were, of course, many varying views and steamy arguments on the matter. Fistfights took place in cafés and homes throughout the island. There was, however, the small group of men and women led by Albizu, who saw the forthcoming referendum as the last chance for Puerto Rico's independence. They knew that the Commonwealth idea would win at the polls. But there was another way to stop it: to murder the man who had brought the idea to reality: Governor Luis Muñoz Marín.

Albizu and seven other Nationalists had been arrested in 1936 after the murder of Police Chief Riggs. Albizu was convicted of "trying to overthrow the federal government in Puerto Rico." He had served seven years in a penitentiary in Atlanta and now was back on the island. His headquarters were in Ponce, his birthplace. On October 29, 1950, a box of detonators was stolen from a building site in Ponce. The night before there had been a prison break. Two guards were killed. One hundred and twelve inmates had escaped, some of them Nationalists.

In San Juan the police stopped a car filled with guns—and Nationalists.

Muñoz was warned. He agreed that riflemen should be placed on two buildings overlooking La Fortaleza. He agreed with Inés that their two young daughters, Viviana and Victoria, should be brought home from school. Otherwise he stuck to his accustomed schedule.

On October 30 his day began as usual at six in the

morning when he entered his large wood-paneled office in the four-centuries-old white fort-castle overlooking the walls of the Old City and the sun-sparked sea. His huge antique mahogany desk was covered, as usual, with high piles of papers. (There were more piles of papers in the bedroom and in the library next to the bedroom. The governor had his own filing system—in his head. "Yes, he would say, "that report is in the library, in the middle of the second pile of papers on the desk chair.")

As usual he spent the morning reading and dictating. Then he had an appointment with Attorney General Geigel-Polanco. He planned to stop, as usual, for a lunch break at noon.

But this day was not as usual.

A black car pulled to a halt before La Fortaleza. Five men jumped out, machine guns blazing. A policeman guarding the entrance shouted out a warning and fell dead.

The Nationalists aimed their machine-gun fire directly at the governor's office on the second floor.

Inés had come into the office. She screamed as a bullet slashed by her. Muñoz and the attorney general pulled her to the floor as bullets crashed into the walls.

Shots seemed to be coming from all over. Was La Fortaleza surrounded?

Muñoz crawled to the window and looked out.

He saw a man lying dead, a machine gun beside him. Another man squirmed and dived under the car for cover. Bullets pierced the car tires. And as the heavy sedan slowly settled over him, the man kept spraying bullets from his hiding place. He was as safe there as in an armored tank.

Muñoz and Inés ran from the office and up the stairs to their apartment on the third floor. There Viviana and Victoria were huddled together behind the four-poster bed, terrified but unhurt.

Muñoz switched on the radio and learned that armed Nationalists were attacking La Fortaleza. "Their strength," said the news reporter "is not yet known."

Police from all over the district converged on the Governor's Palace. Four of the Nationalists were killed. The other, under the car, kept shooting. But by one o'clock he was wounded. The shooting was over at La Fortaleza.

But there were other terrorist uprisings throughout the island. Thirty-three people were killed.

By evening all known Nationalists were rounded up and imprisoned. But two days later two of Albizu's men in Washington, D.C., shot at President Truman. A guard was killed, but the President was not hurt.

The people of Puerto Rico went to the polls to register as scheduled. They voted for the Commonwealth. Then they elected delegates to a constitutional convention. For six months these ninety-two men and women hammered away at a new Puerto Rican constitution. On March 3, 1952, the people of the island voted on it. The new constitution was overwhelmingly accepted on the island and ratified in Washington. On July 25, 1952, exactly fifty-four years after U.S. troops had taken the island from Spain, the Commonwealth of Puerto Rico was proclaimed.

It was a momentous day, made the more memorable with parades and U.S. Air Force planes flying in formation overhead. At four P.M. Governor Luis Muñoz Marín raised the flag of Puerto Rico—five red and white stripes with a lone white star on a blue triangle. And as the flag flapped in the wind over the ancient El Morro fortress in Old San Juan, mayors in seventy-seven municipalities throughout the island raised the flag in a simultaneous salute: a salute to a new kind of government.

The people of this Caribbean island had voted by a 4½-to-1 majority that they wished to be a Commonwealth or, as the constitution phrased it (in Spanish): a "free associated state" of the United States. The island's self-rule, sought so long ago by Muñoz Rivera, now was complete. The United States Congress could no longer alter or affect the laws made in and for the Commonwealth of Puerto Rico.

Under the guidance, inspiration, and driving force of Governor Luis Muñoz Marín, the island, once known as "the Poorhouse of the Caribbean," was now known as "the Showplace of the Caribbean." During the 1950's leaders from over 125 developing countries in Asia, Africa, and Latin America came to Puerto Rico to study the many new techniques Muñoz and his followers had developed in solving Puerto Rico's economic and social problems, to see the results of Operation Bootstrap. Muñoz, therefore, had an influence which spread far beyond his own small sun-soaked island.

Despite the fact he had become something of a world figure, Don Luis retained the simplicity of dress and manner, the informality, the easy camaraderie, and warm humor of the days when he traveled through the cities, the *barrios*, the seaside villages, and the mountains trying to persuade people to put their names on a petition so that the new Popular Party could appear on the ballot.

Though he had no time now to write poetry, he was nevertheless known by his countrymen as *El Vate* (the Bard). Reporters called him the Poet-Politician. He was a unique blend of the practical, pragmatic, dynamic *posibilista* and the compassionate, sensitive, and soulful poet. His brilliant speeches often reflected these opposite sides of his nature. For example, in a speech on the complexities of the status issue and the constitution, he suddenly slipped into a description of the island which was poetry:

> To the Puerto Rican, *patria* [country] is the colors of the landscape, the change of seasons, the smell of the earth wet with fresh rain, the voice of the streams, the crash of the ocean against the shore, the fruits, the songs, the habits of work and leisure, the typical dishes for special occasions and the meager ones for everyday, the flowers, the valleys and the pathways. But even more than these things, *patria* is the people. . . .

Even the governor's most businesslike memos could be poetic—in content. One morning he issued the following "petition" in respect of a small, sparrowlike bird called a *reinita* which had built its nest in the huge cut glass chandelier above his office desk. He feared that the nest might be dislodged if someone slammed the office door:

TO: WHOEVER IS GOING TO CLOSE THIS DOOR

FROM: LUIS MUÑOZ MARÍN

PLEASE DO NOT CLOSE THIS DOOR. IF YOU DO, YOU WILL DEPRIVE THE REINITA WHO LIVES IN THE CHANDELIER AT THE CENTER OF THE ROOM OF HER LEGALLY ESTABLISHED HOME.

I BEG YOU, THEREFORE, TO PLEASE LEAVE THIS DOOR OPEN.

By the time the 1960 election campaign came along, Muñoz was so beloved by his people, so widely respected throughout the world, that no one thought it would be necessary for him to do any campaigning—until a Sunday morning in September, when he was suddenly and unexpectedly faced with the worse crisis in his political career; a crisis which could well mean the end of his political career and an end of the *Populares* as a party.

On that Sunday morning, September 3, thousands of priests in Catholic churches all through the land read out a letter signed by the two American bishops of Puerto Rico. The message was short, simple, and very clear: The philosophy of the Popular Party was "based on the modern heresy that the people's will and not the divine law decides what is moral and immoral." The Popular Party was anti-Church and anti-Catholic. Therefore anyone who voted for any Popular candidate would be excommunicated!

Why?

Muñoz himself was not much of a churchgoer. But he was fundamentally a deeply religious man. One day his good friend Antonio Colorado had said to him, "Don

Luis, I don't deny that there is a God. I simply don't know."

And Muñoz answered, "Antonio, don't be stupid. There *must* be a God. Everything speaks of it."

He was religious. And like 90 percent of his countrymen, he was a Catholic. But he was not an orthodox Catholic. And he knew that overpopulation was a real problem.

In speech after speech he brought out the stark statistics of the overpopulation of the island and the impossible problems the ever-soaring birthrate brought.

"It is interesting to note," he said, "that in Puerto Rico the birthrate is forty per one thousand, whereas in the continental United States it is twenty-two per thousand. If, during the past ten years, Puerto Rico had had the same birthrate as the United States, unemployment would have practically disappeared by this time."

He pointed out repeatedly that with all the efforts to create more jobs, better education, better housing, and better health for the people of Puerto Rico, there was one insurmountable stumbling block in every area: the small land of Puerto Rico was one of the most heavily populated places on earth—2,500,000 people on an island 35 miles wide and 100 miles long. And, with the Church's strict ban against birth control, the population figures kept swelling every year. "The island's troubles are a problem in multiplication," Muñoz said. "Or, as an economist put it, 'We have to run like hell to stand still.' "

The bishops answered Muñoz in a word: excommunication. And to offer the voters an alternative, they formed the Christian Action Party. They would bring the birth control fight straight to the polls.

Never before had any politician in a Catholic country run for office against such odds. Any man or woman who voted for any Popular candidate would be condemned to eternal damnation.

How to campaign against this?

"We must not attack the Church," Muñoz told the party leaders. In his first speech after the bishops' edict he gave the keynote, which was carried out through the next two months of the election campaign. "I am not running for bishop," he told the crowd. "I don't know anything about the job. And the bishops should not run for governor. They know religion. I know politics. Continue being a religious person. But religion is something separate from politics. Don't let the bishops tell you how to vote."

But across the country, priests were preaching the message of the bishops. At least, many priests were. There were some who refused to read the excommunication letter. Others asked their congregation to leave the church for five minutes and then read the bishop's letter to the empty pews. In some churches when the priest started to preach about the *Populares* and excommunication, most of the congregation got up and walked out.

Yet across the country it was clear that the people were torn by conflict. Would they vote for the Christian Action Party? Would they stay away from the polls on election day?

They came to the polls. Muñoz won 68 percent of the

votes. And the Popular Democratic candidates across the island won seventy-six of the seventy-seven districts.

During the next four years as governor Don Luis came to be regarded by his people as a sort of superhero. The credit for Puerto Rico's amazing statistics was laid at his feet.

- A greater percentage of the people came to the polls in Puerto Rico than in any other country in the Western Hemisphere. And honesty was now an election byword.
- Puerto Rico now spent more money per person on education than any other nation in the world except Israel. Literacy had climbed from less than 50 percent, when Muñoz first ran, to 86 percent. Ninety-four percent of the children of grade-school age attended school. On the Mainland the figure was 96 percent.
- The island's per person income was one of the fastest growing in the world.
- Puerto Rico's public health service was one of the best in the hemisphere. The average life expectancy had risen to seventy years, equaling that of the Mainland. The death rate was 7.5 per thousand, lower than on the Mainland. Malaria, once a scourge of the island, had been wiped out. The death rate from tuberculosis was almost at the low level it had reached in the United States.
- New factories were being built at the rate of 100 a year.
- The government goal of providing every Puerto Rican family with a good home had reached an incredible halfway mark. Most of these homes were the so-called

"self-help house" made of cement blocks with a living-dining room, two bedrooms, and a bathroom. With a government technician to guide them, groups of 50 to 100 families pooled their free labor and put up the houses. Each cost its owner about $400 and was paid for over ten years in small installments. Most families eventually added a kitchen and more bedrooms. In the cities, slum dwellers were moved by the thousands to new low-income public housing developments.

• New roads ribboned the land. An islandwide network of telephone wires striped the sky. Water pipes and electric-power lines ribbed the earth, reaching every town and village.

Sisyphus had shoved the boulder up the mountain, and it clearly would not crash down again.

But there was one problem. Don Luis (no one called him "the Governor") was sixty-six years old. He had served for four terms—sixteen years. What would happen if . . . when . . . ?

It was something no one wanted to speak about or think about. And, after all, Don Luis was still the same hardworking, easygoing, strong, yet gentle, informal, warm, and friendly man he had always been. He was sixty-six years young. There was no problem. Not yet.

But Luis Muñoz Marín did not agree.

The people had to be convinced that it was they—not he—who had made this island success story. It was they—not he—who could and would carry the story forward.

Before the Popular Party Nominating Convention of

1964, Muñoz sent a letter to all the delegates, asking whether he should retire. Ninety percent said no.

The delegates—9,000 of them—met on a Sunday afternoon in Isidora García Baseball Park in the city of Mayagüez. At eleven o'clock Don Luis stood up to speak. He was met with a veritable wall of applause and cheers.

When they quieted, finally, he thanked them. And he said that the same faith they had in him—he had in them. "It is *you* who have wrought the miracles on this island!" he shouted. "It is *your* strength that will keep the people of Puerto Rico going onward—up the hill! You don't need *me*."

Suddenly a visible wave of shock and horror went through the crowd. There had been rumors that Muñoz would not run again. But no one would believe them. What was he telling them now?

"I am not leaving you. I am returning to you."

Then they understood what he was saying. "No!" they screamed out. Nine thousand men and women with one voice. "NO!"

He held up his hands for silence. But they could not be silent. Some were crying; some were waving their hands at him, four fingers raised: four more years! All were shouting. "Four years more! Four years more!"

His wife, Doña Inés, ran to the microphone. "Please!" she pleaded. "Let him speak!"

"No!" they shouted. They screamed, "We don't accept it! *No renuncie! No renuncie!* Don't resign!"

Doña Felisa, the mayor of San Juan, came to the microphone. "Please," she pleaded, "This is what

Muñoz wants. This is what he feels is best for Puerto Rico. As much as we feel we cannot go on without him, we must go along with his wishes. Please. Please. We have to help him at this moment."

They would not listen. They did not want to hear.

But Doña Felisa was the head of the San Juan Delegation. Next to Muñoz she was the most respected political figure on the island.

Presently, the weeping, screaming delegates quieted down.

"Muñoz wants to show us," she said, "that we *can* go on without him. He is doing it to teach us. And we must accept it."

Then Doña Inés spoke once more, spoke quietly now, and now they listened. "You owe it to him. And to yourselves. Let him step down. Let him live."

That evening Doña Inés and Don Luis drove through the city of Mayagüez on their way to the airport. The Puerto Rican flag and the party flag hung everywhere: the party flag white, with the *jíbaro* in his *pava,* red. The symbol Antonio Colorado had drawn in the office of *La Democracia* two decades ago.

Mayagüez: the city of the Popular Party Nominating Convention. Huge posters had been pasted up on walls and store windows: WELCOME MUÑOZ.

Now, in the evening, the streets were crowded with people, waving, weeping. "*Adiós,* Don Luis," they called. "Muñoz . . . good-bye."

Afterword

Although Muñoz had refused to run for governor in 1964, he did agree to run for Senator at Large. But after two years he left the post, indeed he left Puerto Rico—for when he was on the scene people kept regarding him as the unofficial governor. The general feeling was that nothing should be done unless Don Luis had been consulted. Since the purpose of his "abdication" had been to show his people that they could get on very well without him, he saw that he would have to stay out of Puerto Rican politics until it was thoroughly proved that other men could fill his shoes.

The first man who tried was Roberto Sánchez Vilella, who had been Muñoz's right-hand man for two decades. Perhaps no one on the island could have successfully stepped into the giant-size shoes of the beloved and brilliant Don Luis. In any case, Sánchez proved somewhat of a disappointment to his countrymen, and although the various programs started under Muñoz continued to do well under Sánchez, the governor was defeated in 1968, as was the Popular Democratic Party, which had split into two factions. Had the party not split they would have won, for the total vote of both factions was larger than that pulled by the NPP—the New Progressive Party—and its leader, Luis Ferré, who was a long time pro-statehood Republican.

Muñoz lived in Rome all during the Ferré years. But he returned in 1972 to campaign for his party and its proposed governor, Rafael Hernández Colón, who had been his protégé. The return of Don Luis was likened to the return of the Messiah. Some 200,000 cheering, weeping, screaming people gathered to meet him when he got off the plane.

He campaigned hard for his party, and for Hernández. But, typically, he stuck to radio. He insisted that Hernández do all the campaigning on TV. To no one's surprise Hernández Colón and the Popular Party won by a landslide in 1972, and his pro-Commonwealth party is still in power.

Most of the innovative programs born in the Muñoz era continue today as an integral part of Puerto Rican life and culture. But the U.S. recession of the 1970's deeply affected and afflicted Puerto Rico, and Operation Bootstray has slowed down. Nevertheless, the per capita income when Bootstrap started was $279 a year. In 1974 it was $2,000 a year.

The birth control programs started by Muñoz continue, but without much effect. The economic problems are made ever more intense by the constantly swelling population. In 1975 there were 3,300,000 people crowded onto the 3,600-square-mile island, 56 percent of which is mountainous. The population density: over 900 people per square mile! (For the United States to have an equal population density every person in the world—over three billion—would have to live within its borders.)

After the 1972 election Luis Muñoz Marín remained on the island and continued to be a vital and respected force in Puerto Rican life. He was, however, careful to avoid the role of "superadviser" in the realms of island programs and politics. In 1973 he accepted the position of chairman of the Puerto Rican Section of the Ad Hoc Advisory Group on Puerto Rico, which was appointed by the U.S. President and the Puerto Rican governor to make recommendations for improving the political relationship between the Commonwealth of Puerto Rico and the United States. In October, 1975, after two years of hearings and study, the Advisory Group submitted its recommendations to President Ford. The report was aimed at improving "Puerto Rico's hopes for regaining its formerly impressive economic momentum and also at consolidating its cultural and political autonomy" in a permanent association with the United States.

Important Dates

1859 Luis Muñoz Rivera born in Barranquitas.

1890 Muñoz Rivera founds his own newspaper, *La Democracia*.

1893 Muñoz Rivera marries Amalia Marín.

1896 Muñoz Rivera goes to Spain to seek self-government for Puerto Rico.

1897 Spain grants Puerto Rico self-government (and Muñoz Rivera is called "The George Washington of Puerto Rico").

1898 Muñoz Rivera elected the first premier of Puerto Rico.
LUIS MUÑOZ MARÍN is born in San Juan.
Spanish-American War; U.S. troops take Puerto Rico.

1900 Foraker Act is passed by U.S. Congress, and Puerto Rico passes from U.S. military to U.S. civilian rule.

1901 Muñoz Rivera takes his family to New York City, where he founds the new English-Spanish newspaper *Puerto Rico Herald*.

1904 Muñoz Rivera helps found the Unionist Party.

1910 Muñoz Rivera goes to Washington, D.C., as resident commissioner, and Luisito enters Georgetown Prep in Washington, D.C.

1916 Muñoz Rivera returns to Puerto Rico, where he dies.

1917 U.S. Congress passes the Jones Bill. Henceforth all Puerto Ricans will be U.S. citizens, and all Puerto Rican men will be given the vote in island elections.

1917 Luis Muñoz Marín goes to Washington as secretary to the new resident commissioner.

1919 Muñoz Marín comes to New York City to found a new literary journal. He meets and marries Muna Lee. The "Greenwich Village period" flourishes.

1920 Their first child, Muna, is born. Muñoz Marín brings his family back to Puerto Rico, where he works for the Socialist Party.

1921 A son, Luis Muñoz Lee, is born in San Juan.

1931 Muñoz Marín and his family return to New York City, where Muñoz becomes widely respected for his brilliant articles on Puerto Rico and other subjects.

1931 Muñoz and his family return to Puerto Rico, where he helps found a new Liberal Party.

1932 Luis Muñoz Marín is elected Senator at Large and goes to Washington, D.C., where he meets President Roosevelt and becomes an influential figure.

1934 Owing in large measure to Muñoz's work, a new federal agency, the Puerto Rico Reconstruction Administration, is formed.

1937 Muñoz and his followers are expelled from the Liberal Party because Muñoz urged that the party boycott the 1936 elections in protest against the proposed Tydings Bill.

1938 Muñoz founds a new party: the Popular Democratic Party.

1940 After a dramatic islandwide struggle, the *Populares* win the election, and Muñoz is elected president of the Puerto Rican Senate.

1940 Muñoz and his party pass twenty-two new bills they hope will better dramatically the life of the islanders.

1941 President Roosevelt appoints Rexford Guy Tugwell as the new U.S. governor of Puerto Rico. Muñoz and Tugwell put twenty-two bills into operation and get Operation Bootstrap under way.

1947 Muñoz and Muna are divorced. Muñoz marries Inés Mendoza.

U.S. Congress amends the Jones Act so that Puerto

Ricans can elect their own governor. Women will be allowed to vote in Puerto Rico for the first time.

1948 Luis Muñoz Marín becomes the first elected governor of Puerto Rico.

1950 In Public Law 600 U.S. Congress recognizes the right of Puerto Ricans to select their own form of government. Muñoz, Inés, and their two daughters, Viviana and Victoria, are targets of assassins' bullets.

1951 In islandwide referendum, 76 percent of Puerto Rican voters select a Commonwealth form of government, and a convention drafts the new constitution.

1952 Governor Muñoz proclaims the founding of the Commonwealth of Puerto Rico. Muñoz is reelected governor.

1956 Muñoz reelected governor.

1960 Muñoz reelected governor, with 68 percent of the votes, despite the fact that two American bishops threaten excommunication for Catholics who voted for Muñoz and his party.

1964 Muñoz refuses to run again as governor but accepts position of Senator at Large.

1966 Muñoz and Inés travel in Europe, live in Rome.

1972 Muñoz returns to Puerto Rico to campaign for Rafael Hernández Colón as governor. Hernández and the Popular party win the election.

1973 Muñoz accepts the position of chairman of the Puerto Rican Section of the ad hoc committee appointed by the U.S. President and the Puerto Rican governor to make recommendations for improving political relations between Puerto Rico and the United States.

Important People

ALBIZU CAMPOS, PEDRO Leader of the Puerto Rican Nationalist Party, the party with Independence for Puerto Rico as its chief political platform.
BARCELÓ ANTONIO Leader of the *Unionista* party, (which Muñoz Rivera had helped to found) and later founder of the Liberal Party.
BLACK, RUBY U.S. journalist, friend of Eleanor Roosevelt. Influential in aiding Puerto Rico in the 1930's.
COLORADO, ANTONIO Author and professor, one of Muñoz Marín's earliest and most dedicated followers.
GRUENING, ERNEST The American director of the Puerto Rican Reconstruction Administration in the 1930's.
IGLESIAS, SANTIAGO Leader of the Puerto Rican Socialist Party in the 1920's. Later joined coalition with Puerto Rican Republican Party, and was sent to Washington D.C. as resident commissioner.
LEE, MUNA Born in Mississippi, a poet, translator, feminist. Married Luis Muñoz Marín in 1919.
MARÍN, AMALIA Married Luis Muñoz Rivera in 1893. Mother of Luis Muñoz Marín.
MENDOZA, INÉS An early disciple of Muñoz Marín, she became his second wife in 1947.
MOSCOSO, TEODORO First director of Puerto Rico's Economic Development Association, known as *Fomento.* It succeeded in "fomenting" many new industries on the island; the backbone of Operation Bootstrap.
MUÑOZ LEE, MUNA Born in 1920; daughter of Muna Lee de Muñoz and Muñoz Marín.

MUÑOZ LEE, LUIS Born in 1921, son of Muna and Muñoz Marín.
MUÑOZ MENDOZA, VICTORIA Youngest daughter of Inés Mendoza de Marín and Muñoz Marín.
MUÑOZ MENDOZA, VIVIANA. Eldest daughter of Inés Mendoza de Muñoz Marín and Muñoz Marín.
MUÑOZ RIVERA, LUIS Famous Puerto Rican statesman, resident commissioner, and father of Luis Muñoz Marín.
PIÑERO, JESÚS The first Puerto Rican governor of the island, appointed by President Truman in 1945.
RIGGS, E. FRANCIS The American Chief of Police in Puerto Rico who was murdered by the Nationalists on Feb. 3, 1936.
RINCÓN, FELISA An early disciple of Muñoz Marín; she became the first woman mayor of San Juan, and the second most important politician on the island.
SAGASTA, PRÁXEDES The Spanish premier, who lived up to promise he had made Luis Muñoz Rivera by granting Puerto Rico self-rule in 1897.
TUGWELL, REXFORD GUY American governor of the island from 1941 to 1945. Tugwell worked closely with Muñoz (then president of the Puerto Rican Senate) and was the most effective American governor the island ever had.

Bibliography

AITKEN, THOMAS H. *Poet in the Fortress.* New York, New American Library, 1964.

BRAU, M. M., *Island in the Crossroads: The History of Puerto Rico.* Garden City, New York, Doubleday and Company 1968.

BROWN, WENZELL, *Dynamite on Our Doorstep: Puerto Rican Paradox.* New York, Greenberg: Publisher, 1945.

EDWARDS, MARY LOUISE, *Love Me, Puerto Rico.* Hato Rey, Puerto Rico, Barton House, 1962.

GLASS, ALEX, publisher and editor, *Puerto Rican Living.* San Juan, Living, Inc., 1970.

GRUBER, RUTH, *Felisa Rincon de Gautier: The Mayor of San Juan.* New York, Thomas Y. Crowell Company, 1972.

———, *Puerto Rico: Island of Promise.* New York. Hill and Wang, 1960.

HANSON, EARL PARKER, *Puerto Rico: Ally for the Progress.* Princeton, New Jersey, D. Van Nostrand Company, 1962.

———, *Puerto Rico, Land of Wonders.* New York, Alfred A. Knopf, 1960.

———, *Transformation: The Story of Modern Puerto Rico.* New York, Simon and Schuster, 1955.

KURTIS, ARLENE HARRIS, *Puerto Ricans, from Island to Mainland.* New York, Julian Messner, 1969.

MANCHESTER, WILLIAM, *The Glory and the Dream.* Boston-Toronto, Little, Brown and Company, 1973.

MATHEWS, THOMAS, *Luis Muñoz Marín: A Concise Biography.* New York, American R.D.M. Corporation, 1967.

———, *Puerto Rican Politics and the New Deal.* Gainesville, Florida, University of Florida Press, 1960.

MOSKIN, J. ROBERT, "Puerto Rico: Island at a Crossroads." In *Look* magazine. New York, Cowles Publisher, March, 1964.

NORRIS, MARIANNA, *Father and Son for Freedom.* New York, Dodd, Mead & Company, 1968.

PAGE, HOMER, *Puerto Rico: The Quiet Revolution.* New York, Viking Press, 1963.

PETRULLO, VINCENZO, *Puerto Rican Paradox.* Philadelphia, University of Pennsylvania Press, 1947.

Puerto Rico U.S.A. Office of the Commonwealth of Puerto Rico, Washington, D.C., December, 1969.

RAND, CHRISTOPHER, *The Puerto Ricans.* New York, Oxford University Press, 1958.

REYNOLDS, MACK, *Puerto Rican Patriot: The Life of Luis Muñoz Rivera.* New York, The Macmillan Company, 1969.

ROLLINS, FRANCES, *Getting to Know Puerto Rico.* New York, Coward-McCann, 1967.

STERLING, PHILIP, and BRAU, MARIA, *The Quiet Rebels.* Garden City, New York, Doubleday and Company, 1968.

WAGENHEIM, KAL and DE WAGENHEIM, OLGA JIMÉNEZ, (editor), *The Puerto Ricans: A Documentary History.* New York, Praeger Publishers, 1973.

Among the numerous speeches by Governor Muñoz Marín used as background information for this book:

"Inaugural Address of the first Governor of Puerto Rico to be Elected by the People: Luis Muñoz Marín, January 2, 1949."

"Message of Luis Muñoz Marín, Governor of Puerto Rico, to the Legislative Assembly: February 23, 1950; March 14, 1951; March 20, 1952; February 7, 1955; January 17, 1957."

"The Deep Significance of United States Citizenship." Address given by Muñoz Marín at the fourth anniversary of the Commonwealth of Puerto Rico, July 25, 1956.

Speech before the Economic Club of Detroit, November 22, 1965.

Index